Roo✝s of a Man

7 Principles For Growing Strong and Powerful

ROOᵗS OF A MAN

7 PRINCIPLES FOR GROWING
STRONG AND POWERFUL

by Dr. Ernest C. Garlington

Book editing and design by Laura A. Marsala
Jacket photograph by Ken Porter

Library of Congress Catalog Number:
ISBN: 1-4196-2172-6

LLIII
Living Legacy III
P.O. Box 597, Marion, CT 06444
Printed in the United States of America

This book is dedicated to all of the men in the hood who want to work hard, get paid and support their families. "Meditate on the Lord's commands day and night and you will be prosperous and successful." (Joshua 1:8)

May men everywhere, from all walks of life, bond together to empower our families and communities.

ACKNOWLEDGMENTS

I thank my Lord and Savior Jesus Christ for all His guidance, protection, mercy, grace and inspiration. I thank Him for the men He has placed in my life to mold me into the man that I am today. My father-in-law, Robert L. Powell Sr., taught me how to be a man and father who guides with strength, dignity and humility. My mentor and chief executive officer, Dr. James Gatling, taught me how to use wisdom, inner-strength and discernment in making decisions. The Rev. Larry Green, of Grace Baptist Church in Waterbury, Conn., is a magnificent preacher and I thank him for not only inspiring me but teaching the Word of God when he preaches. My Christian mentor, Bob Jacks, taught me how to bring men to Christ. My college coach at Holy Cross, Mark Duffner, taught me how to be a champion with a warrior spirit. My big brother, Larry Garlington, taught me from birth what it is to be a man who sacrifices for his family and he provided the roots and foundation that allowed me to benefit from the guidance of all the men who have shaped my life. Larry has more integrity and faith than any man I know. My son, Derek Hopson Garlington, has taught me how to love in ways beyond my human understanding. When he hurts, I am in pain; when he has joy, I am ecstatic. Every time I experience the love of my son, I strengthen my Christian walk.

Men in my Inner Circle

Will Bradford III • *Joe Foy II* • *Erik Patchkofsky*
James Perry, Ph.D. • *Robert Powell Jr.*
Omar Ramirez • *Shawn Robinson* • *Melvin White Jr.*

The women in my life have been phenomenal. My mother, Laura Garlington, was the first Black teacher in Waterbury and taught me to value education. She loves me unconditionally and demonstrates tremendous devotion and commitment to her children. My mother-in-law, Leanna Powell, is my friend and mother. She not only supports me in all that I do, she loves me enough to challenge me when I'm wrong. My sister, Castella Murphy, has strong faith in Jehovah and her prayers help sustain me. Karyn Berkley is not only my wife Darlene's best friend since childhood, but is a best friend to me as well. My daughter, Dotteanna Garlington, has a love of family that has bonded us and taught me how important it is to spend family time. Her focus and determination in college inspires me. As Jalen grows into womanhood, I hope to make her proud. My wife, Dr. Darlene Powell-Garlington, is my life. She is the woman God chose for me. She is my Queen, a *Proverbs 31* wife and a virtuous woman. My greatest mission in life is to protect and provide for her, our children and family.

TABLE OF CONTENTS

CHAPTER FOUR: Eliminating the Weeds and Poison Vines: Combating Oppression, Racism and Self-Destructive Behavior

CHAPTER FIVE: Sunshine Sweetens Your Fruit: Creating Joy and Happiness Through Relationships & Family

CHAPTER SIX: Money Tree: Nurturing Your Financial Power

CHAPTER SEVEN: Tree of Life: Harvesting Your Divine Destiny

AUTHOR'S NOTE

Men,

I pray that this book touches your spirit and ignites your faith. I wrote it out of genuine love for you because of the experiences we share as Black men and as children of God. I offer this information to you because of my respect for you, our destiny together, and our covenant with the Lord. It is my hope that this book will inspire and motivate you to take decisive steps toward your vision and dreams.

We are first and foremost God's creation in his image. Because of God's love for us, I feel a sense of invincibility and nothing can come between me and His divine purpose for my life. A large part of that purpose is to motivate you as Black men to find God within you, enable you to know yourself, help you realize your own divine purpose and reveal to you that your faith in the Lord will give you the power to triumph over all your circumstances.

As African American men, we share a rich and proud history. America has been built on the backs of our forefathers. We have made the United States the most powerful and wealthiest nation in the world from the sweat and blood of 400 years of free slave labor. It's only fitting that, in the eyes of the Lord, we share in what we have created. This is our country! We deserve our part of this nation's inheritance. We must be comfortable in the home that we built and bask in its riches. This is our God-given right. Turn your wounds into weapons of mass determination!

I hope the words written on these pages will help you reclaim that right. Poverty is the root of all evil and the greatest challenge to the African American male since slavery. Our faithful and relentless pursuit of excellent education and employment is the key to conquering poverty. We must transform ourselves, our countrymen and our nation to elevate the Christian spirit of America. I implore you to pray about this daily. Believe it in your heart, spirit, mind and soul. I pray I can help you realize who we are as Black men, especially in Our Father, Christ. We are warriors of God. Only a warrior of God could survive the genocide of the middle passage and the demonic atrocities of slavery. Like Jesus Christ, our forefathers have awakened from the crucifixion of the middle passage. Our faith is what allowed us to survive. We are a blessed people because, according to His word, those who have faith will be blessed according to that faith.

There is a Holy War raging within the spirit of our people and it's up to us to claim the victory. Our faith has been terrorized by poverty, self-destructive behavior and oppression. Take action toward your divine destiny. "Seek ye first the kingdom of God, and his righteousness; and all these things shall be added unto you" *(Matthew 6:33)*. Power, inner strength, joy and prosperity will drive you to provide for your family and bring your dreams to fruition.

I hope these words I impart to you will succeed in helping you increase your faith and inspire you to develop a deeper spiritual connection with your Creator so that you can begin to enjoy all of the blessings that are rightfully yours.

Use this straightforward, prescriptive guide to help you fulfill your purpose in life. The message in this book is simple and clear. The most important part of the battle is within, and you already have the tools you need to win. The Lord has given the African American male the opportunity to gain power over his life and to acquire great wealth in order to uplift our people in America, the Caribbean, Africa and all over the world.

As you involve yourself in these pages, know that I am taking this spiritual journey with you. As you reach your divine purpose, you allow me to reach mine. Meditate on the Lord's commands day and night, and you will be prosperous and successful *(Joshua 1:8)*. May these words be a blessing in the name of our Lord and Savior, Jesus Christ.

Love and Power,

Ernest Garlington

Ernest C. Garlington, Ph.D.

HOW TO MAKE THE MOST OF THIS BOOK

*Each chapter begins with self-assessment statements,
numbered 1-5, related to the principle theme
being addressed. Think about how you feel
regarding each statement.*

*Following the assessment statements is a set of
open-ended personal inventory questions to be completed
by the reader. Respond to each question based on your
views and experiences and write in your answers.*

*After completing this task, assess your answers and
review them again after reading the chapter.*

CHAPTER ONE

Planting the Seed: Understanding Identity Development and Family of Origin Influences

PLANTING THE SEED: ASSESSMENT STATEMENTS

Not at all				Very much
1	2	3	4	5

1. I have a strong relationship with God.

2. I have well-defined goals and dreams.

3. I have a support network to help me reach my goals.

4. Conscious decisions that I make positively impact other African American males.

5. I have a sense of purpose in my life.

PLANTING THE SEED: PERSONAL INVENTORY

1. My vision for my life is:

2. The most important values in my life are:

3. Five characteristics that describe me are:

4. My family history affects my identity by:

5. An African American man who has power over his life is:

NOTE: You will find inventory questions throughout this book. Please take advantage of the space left open to you to jot down your own notes and personal thoughts as you move through the text. You may find it helpful to review your notes from time to time to assess your progress or revisit an idea at a later date.

THE SPIRITUAL ROOTS OF MEN

I knew.

I knew that my way would be blocked long before my legs carried me to this place.

I surmised correctly, that the forces of doubt would rage as I entered its space.

I was not wanted. Nor was I expected.

Troublesome treks from years past had left me vulnerable and unprotected.

Ahhh, but I'm newly arrived.

Content in knowing who I'm not, but most importantly, just who I am,

An enlightened force that must be reckoned with in this vast, prodigious land.

Fashioned by the Creator, emboldened by my Maker,

I've learned much and am ready to serve.

Ready to receive the kind of power that awaits me, and is found,

In the spiritual roots of men.

— **Larry Toussaint Garlington**

GET GOD, GET STARTED

Are you ready for a change? Of course you are. But, in case you're wondering where you should start, start with God. Your ability to make improvements in your life is directly related to your relationship with God's son, Jesus Christ. We'll explore this further and develop a plan of action to accomplish this later, but for now, just know that the stronger the relationship, the more resources you have available to you. That shouldn't be a surprise. After all, God has the entire universe at His fingertips. Our desires, no matter how great we perceive them, are truly small in His sight. In fact, God wants more for us than we can even fathom. In other words, our brains don't have the capacity to think of the things that God can do for us. Now that's real power, and this knowledge alone should help you realize that if you can dream it, you can achieve it.

As you think about what you plan to do and where you want to go, always consider God first. Let Him be a constant source of inspiration for you and you'll stay on course. Instead of trying to map out your vision, let the Holy Spirit drive your vision for you. Be open to hearing His word through people and prayer. Start paying attention to the messages that are surfacing in your life. God is always communicating with us; now it's time for you to listen to Him.

It's important to understand, however, that our reason for being on this earth is not to solely fulfill our own wishes but to ultimately do God's will. So as situations unfold in our lives, it's important that we not become discouraged. According to *Romans 8:28*, "all things work together for good to those who love God." Even our darkest moments are opportunities for God to turn our trials into triumphs or transform our stumbling blocks into stepping stones. God has a purpose for your life and He sometimes uses experiences to reveal His true intentions to you. I didn't grow up in the church, but I was able to discover my purpose in life by reading the Bible, staying prayerful, and learning to depend on Him for guidance and strength. I suggest that you do the same and I guarantee that you'll come to know why God placed you in this time and space.

But there's more. A solid relationship with God will provide you with a spiritual identification, meaning that you and everyone around you will know that the almighty has your back. Your spirituality communicates to whom you belong as a child of God. And when God is in your corner, the Bible says that no weapon formed against you shall prosper. You're already on the road to change with that knowledge alone. Yet, there are other elements of your identification that you need to explore.

Your identity communicates who you belong to, who you are, what you know, who you know, and how you view the world. The formula looks like this:

**Your ID = Spirituality + Family + Education
+ Social/Economic Status + Society's Effect on Me**

But knowing the formula is only half the battle. In this chapter, we'll discuss how these elements work together and how you can alter them to formulate the seed you need. Then, once we clearly identify your starting point, we'll determine the best place for you to plant this seed to ensure growth.

As demonstrated in the formula, the relationships you forged with your parents, grandparents, siblings, aunts, uncles, and other influencers should be your next point of focus. These people also shape your identity.

UOICE OF EHPERIENCE #1

Tyrone did well in school, but he was under a lot of pressure. In school, the teachers praised him for his grades and motivation. However, when he went home, there was always a problem to deal with. His mother was stressed that Tyrone's older brother Earl kept getting into trouble.

His younger sister had lupus and his mom was constantly taking her to the doctor. It was difficult to study at home and money was tight. Tyrone's boys kept telling him if he'd help them out, they would throw him a few dollars. The few dollars they had in mind was more than Tyrone's mother earned in a month working as a teacher's aid. His mother had always encouraged him to work hard in school and Tyrone felt good when he made her proud by making the honor roll. When he was in the streets, he played down his academic achievements and focused on presenting the bravado attitude that kept people off him. Most of his friends thought they were gangsta and didn't even go to school.

One path Tyrone might have taken: *The pressures were mounting and Tyrone decided to help his boys out just one time. Most of them were in fights over turf and killing each other.*

He would have no part of that. They also sold drugs in their community. He wouldn't sell drugs either. Well, not really. All he had to do was drop off the package and bring back the cash, no big deal, he thought. (Anxiety and guilt were chasing him, but he ran too fast to let them catch up.) He moved quickly through the back streets to avoid traffic and was able to complete the job in record time. His experience on the track team was a plus and before he even had a chance to consider the consequences, Tyrone was "helping out" on a regular basis.

That is, until he was caught during a raid after one of his boys sold to an undercover cop. During the raid, one of the officers was shot and killed. Everyone's sentence was harsh. Jail time was hard. Tyrone tried to stay focused on his studies, but it wasn't the same as school. When his mother visited, she seemed more depressed than angry. She had really aged.

Several years later, Tyrone was back living with his mother and looking for a job. His record kept being a problem. What did his parole officer expect him to do, work at a fast food chain? Tyrone spent his days hanging out with the fellas shooting pool and his nights with one of his several lady friends. His dreams of being an architect long gone, he played around with the idea of being a rap artist.

He had the stories to tell and the lyrics and beat to go with it. There were rap artists who shared his experiences of living the hard life in the streets. It was difficult trying to break into the game and he didn't have the cash to make a demo CD.

Although he had never touched drugs while selling, Tyrone began to get high in order to deal with his frustration and feelings of hopelessness. He felt that the system was always going to keep the Black man down.

The other path Tyrone might have taken: *He wanted to please his mother and be the strong Black man that she kept telling him he was capable of being. But, the pull to be part of the crew that he hung out with was strong. Their focus was on making fast money and hanging with fast women. Some days, Tyrone wondered who he really was and what his future would be.*

He did so well academically that he was accepted into a private school. His guidance counselor encouraged and guided him, and his mother's belief in him was his inspiration. Tyrone's friends teased him about changing into a "boushie negro," but they still showed him respect. In fact, a couple of them had pulled him aside and told him that they were proud of him and that he needed to do some good for the rest of them.

Tyrone was motivated by his dream to give back to his community and make a difference. Although he never admitted it to his mother, her prayers and forcing him to go to church on Easter made a difference. She always encouraged him to go, but he would refuse and she would let it go. But not on Easter Sunday, when she would practically drag him out of bed.

He never quite understood why it was so important to her. She would always take him around, introducing him to the whole church and telling them how well he was doing in school. Despite his protests, Tyrone felt good that his mother viewed him as smart and capable and that she wanted all of her church friends to know it.

Tyrone was able to work hard and go on to college and graduate school. Many of his friends ended up in jail but he always tried to lift them up when they came home and never forgot where he came from. A strong part of his identity was to give hope to other brothers and offer support to those who really wanted to change.

As an architect, Tyrone focused on community development and affordable low-income housing. He was able to purchase a home for his mother and frequently takes her to church on Sunday.

VOICE OF EXPERIENCE #2

Mike was from an all-Black neighborhood in Long Island, New York. He pulled himself up by his own bootstraps. Mike confused having a strong sense of identity as an African American male versus being an African American male obsessed with materialism and selfishness. He came from a strong family within a working-class Black neighborhood, with positive role models around him. His par-

ents did not go to college. They were hardworking people and made sure that Mike and his siblings had everything that they could provide. Mike did well in school, excelled in sports, and went to college. He graduated and went to work for a corporation. Mike continued to do well. He always felt that in order to get something in life, you must work hard, and if you don't work hard you will never get anywhere. As he began to improve financially, he was losing something. He was slowly beginning to forget where he came from. Mike spoke about what he wanted to do as a strong Black man and most people would describe him as a strong Black man. He excelled in business and talked to kids about working hard. However, sometimes he would say things such as, "You know the problem with brothers is they just don't want to work." Slowly but surely, Mike stopped going by the community center. However, he still hung out with Blacks. He hadn't lost identity as being "Black" but he had lost his sense of community and a sense of where he came from. If you were to ask Mike what made the difference between him and the other brothers in the hood and why he was so successful, he would say, "Well, I just wanted to work hard, and I think many of my brothers don't want to work as hard." He started to believe that, rather than feel that he was fortunate to have had good direction and opportunity. Mike had grown up in the church, but felt he didn't really need church anymore because he didn't want to give away all the money he was making. Soon, Mike was making well over six figures. The draw to material things was like a sweet glass of wine and pretty soon, Mike was so high on himself that he had no foundation and had totally forgotten where he came from. He moved to an affluent suburb and had acquired the American dream, but he was losing himself. One day, his grandfather said to him, "You have grown up to be one special Negro."

Mike paused, then and asked, "What are you talking about?" He knew that for the last couple of years he had stopped going back to the community. He didn't attempt to help anybody. Mike was into himself, his new Mercedes, and connecting with other people who had money. He had simply forgotten how he got there. The great thing about this family and being connected with his family was that in that statement, his grandfather began to bring him back and Mike made every attempt to go back into the community. Within one year, Mike was volunteering three times a week tutoring kids in the neighborhood where he grew up.

Mike talked with his grandfather, who asked Mike to come to church. He went to church and he had not heard the gospel choir sing in nearly four years. He remembered what he had lost. When the choir sang his favorite song, he felt like Jesus was talking to him and he silently wept. Every Sunday that gospel choir and that preacher telling him what he could do to strengthen his life and improve his condition motivated and inspired him to become a top executive. He remembered how all of the women praised him in the church and told him he was such a handsome young man and how positive everybody in the community was about him. This is what gave him the strength to move forward. When he came home, his spirit was replenished. He didn't realize that he had become empty trying to fill his spirit with material things. It had never worked. He was searching for happiness and searching for an identity that was false. He realized that he could continue to be a successful person, but his real identity was back at home, helping the community. Mike was really becoming more and more successful at his job, but he was also becoming a community leader whom everyone respected. He was a person who now was viewed as going out in the world, becoming successful and coming back to help develop his community to support the people still living there.

FOCUS ON YOUR FAMILY

How many times have you heard yourself say something and remember how your mom or dad used to say the exact same thing under similar circumstance? Or, maybe you notice that other people tell you how much you remind them of your father or mother. This is no accident or coincidence. Your family history is a critical factor in your life because the people and situations that influenced you when you were growing up affect you today. Family is the foundation of God's covenant community. The specific experiences that you encountered were divinely designed specifically for you so they could help you develop into the man that you are in this moment. Long before your parents conceived you, God knew where you would be born, when you would be born and the parents who would serve as stewards over you during your formative years. Your race, creed, color, hair texture, body form, skin tone, and other features were also predetermined. So, even if there are aspects of your childhood that you don't like, know that God provided you with everything you needed to succeed. The key is to be able to use this information to get the results you want.

Connecting with your past as it relates to your family may help you gain a clearer understanding of why you are where you are today and where you'll be tomorrow unless you commit to change. It's important that you think about the things that you were taught, identify any negative problems or issues that may be holding you back, and start implementing good habits that will propel you to success.

To illustrate the point, we'll use my family origin as an example. I grew up very poor in a home that was infested with rats and roaches. My mom was a single parent and my father was absent for the majority of my childhood. As in many other Black families, my grandmother also largely contributed to my development. She helped raise us and assisted in the cooking, cleaning, and organizing the household while my mother worked. She lived with us until she died when I was sixteen years old. My brother, Larry, and my sisters, Tawanda and Castella, also lived in our household. All of these people had a significant role in my development.

One of my earliest memories is being four years old and we were evicted from an apartment. I stood on the sidewalk with my belongings while my mother looked for help and a place to stay. This was one of the many evictions over the next few years because of my mother's refusal to go on welfare. She was an educated teacher and desired to work. However, the overwhelming burden of taking care of her four children, elderly mother, and two nephews interfered with her career. In addition, the environment at that time was not supportive of the first Black teacher in my hometown of Waterbury, Connecticut. The difficulties took an emotional toll on my mother. Even when we did have a roof over our heads, there were times when my sister and I were so cold that we could see our breath in the cold air. Most days we didn't know what we would eat that day.

The feelings of loss, confusion and frustration from being evicted and living in poverty-stricken conditions inspired me to dream. Throughout my childhood and as a young adult I would dream about a brick and stone house. Stone represented strength and stability. It was a beautiful, large and inviting house that I would escape to in my dreams.

As an adult, I was able to design and have this house built. My present home is like the one I imagined ever since I was four years old. God blessed me further by allowing me to discover that my property on which the house sits has stone ledge. While clearing this land, I found truckloads of stone, which I used to design and build walls, replicating those in my childhood dreams, a fantasy my mother helped foster.

My mom showed me that I could accomplish anything if I had a strong desire and worked hard. When I think about her, the images bring a lot of "can do" stories to mind. If roles were being cast for a story called, "The little woman that dared and did," my mother would have a starring role. She was the only African American in her class at Central Connecticut's Teachers' College.

These feats were accomplished amidst a host of threats and other distractions. Beyond that, my mother raised two nephews, William and Douglas, alongside her own four children, was the primary caretaker of her sister, who was born deaf, and a friend and nurse to her aging mother. I can honestly say that she lives life according to God's will.

During the riots of the late 1960s, around the time of Martin Luther King Jr.'s assassination, my mother's photo ran in the newspapers throughout the country because she helped a white store owner sweep up debris after his business had been vandalized. Although she'd been a victim of racism many times over, she didn't want anyone else to be subjected to the ugliness of racism, even if the victim was white.

Despite my mother's fearless quest for equal rights, she didn't believe that good, honest working people should be punished for the injustices experienced by minorities. My mother saw the store owner as a human being in need and that's why she helped him.

GOLDEN LADY

DEDICATED TO MY MOTHER, LAURA GARLINGTON

You're such a helpful lady
A golden Lady
A passion filled, grand and genuine, kind of lady
An endearing, honest, and fair lady
As quick to praise a stranger, as you would a lifelong friend
You're a blessed lady
A thankful lady
A child rearing, God fearing, spiritual kind of lady
Kindness of heart
Wonderful and dark
Your days will be remembered, and your ways revere

You're an impact lady
An assertive lady
A trailblazing, pioneering, groundbreaking kind of lady
A galvanizing, energizing, and persistent lady
Destined to succeed and determined to make a difference
You're a freedom fighter lady
A civil rights lady
One of the first to wear your hair short and natural kind of lady
A front-line lady
A grass roots lady
Steady as steel
Ready and real
And miles ahead of your time

You're an educated lady
An intelligent lady
A smart, eloquent, and learned lady
Ever willing to lend an ear, or when needed,
A word
You're an unsung lady
A patient lady
A spectacularly modest and humble kind of lady
True to your convictions
Enriching and uplifting
All of whom came your way
Such a captivating lady
An autumn lady
A colorful, cool, and wholesome kind of lady
Gorgeous in your day
Though aging and gray
Your beauty remains now and anew

As so you are, that rarest of ladies
The kind that gives more than she receives, daily
An honorable, up-right and righteous lady
Never discriminating
Always illuminating
And golden.

— **Larry Toussaint Garlington**

Perhaps my mother got many of her qualities from my grandmother. Despite being a double amputee and being confined to a wheelchair, people would still come to her for comfort and strength. Can you imagine that? She never saw herself as a victim or an unfortunate soul. Instead, she focused on the positive. Her attitude naturally drew people in her direction. They came to her for comfort, advice or prayer. She'd provide friends, neighbors and strangers with a shoulder to cry on or a loving hug. Faith was the rock of her foundation and her optimistic thinking was so powerful that it was contagious.

Ironically, people relied on my grandmother for direction even though she wasn't educated in the traditional sense. Her education ended abruptly when she was in the third grade because she had to take on more responsibility on the home front. She assisted her mother in the kitchen and her brothers in the field. This affected her deeply in many ways because she truly valued education. Her verbal skills suffered as a result of her lack of education but because she was so widely respected in the community, people barely noticed. We children were nearly unaware of it, as evidenced by the fact that we came to know her beloved teacher as "Fesser" Lane, not realizing until many years later that what my grandmother meant was "Professor Lane." Still, we loved our grandmother, affectionately known as "Tooie." Born in 1898, she died in 1986, but only after sharing her precious wisdom and her most prized gift: the magic of prayer.

My brother, Larry, also largely impacted my development. He was and continues to be my biggest fan and protector. I definitely looked upon him more as a father than a brother. I remember how much my brother influenced my decision to try out for the neighborhood football team and the impact that had and continues to have on my life. At ten years old, I played football in the playground with the other neighborhood kids. But Darius Butler, an adult who served as the community mentor and also ran the local recreation center, inspired kids to play ball on an organized team. He encouraged me in particular to try out for the local football team, the Waterbury Knights. So when I mentioned this to my brother, I got his full support and he took me to the team tryouts.

My brother and I took a cab to Kennedy High School, which is located in the west end of Waterbury. During the ride, my brother kept telling me how great I was going to do and I wholeheartedly believed him. As you might imagine, tryouts were very competitive and physically taxing. The selection took place over a three-week process in which the kids endured three hours of training on a daily basis in the hot burning sun. More than 200 kids tried out, but only about 40 were selected. In the running back's position, the one I went out for, there were about 30 kids trying out, but the team only kept five. Someone got cut every day. At times there were kids who probably should have made the team, but because of a bad practice on a particular day, they were out. To make the team, you had to beat out the other kids in everything from speed, power, and intellect (yes, playing organized sports does require you to outsmart the opposing team). For young kids, this type of competitive environment can be stressful.

I made the team. It was one of the most memorable days in my life. At an early age, I proved to myself that I could compete and excel. It was also my first opportunity to be part of a real team and that day lead to more opportunities and friends than I could ever count. At the time, the coaches were very impressed with my performance and they provided me with a lot of positive feedback. As I look back, I wish there were more opportunities for Black males to receive positive attention. It felt great to hear the coaches call my name and tell me that I was going to be the star of the team. I scored a few touchdowns during the practice and that was pretty exciting. I remember breaking a touchdown for about 80 yards. I broke two of them on the same day. You're lucky to get a run like that one time during the whole season and many players never achieve such a feat.

Although I was very excited and motivated to play, my brother was happier than I was. Just having him there for support was important. Although he was just eight years older, his maturity was well beyond his years and he was always willing to give advice. At the time of my tryouts, he was just 18 years old, but he taught me that if I worked hard, focused and listened to the instructions from my coaches, I would play well. He was right. I did go on to play very well and our team went undefeated that year. I broke a lot of the touchdown records and a lot of the rushing records. One of the things I most remember is the interest people would show me at the end of the game. "You played a great game," they'd say. But my brother was more concerned about me than how I did. He wanted to be sure that I hadn't suffered any injuries. This spoke volumes to me because it communicated that my value as a human being was not directly connected to how well I performed.

Since I excelled at the game of football, my name was in the newspaper very often and my community was very proud. I was featured in the newspaper every football season from 10 years old until I graduated college. That's how people in the community began to know me. On a regular basis, they expressed that they were proud of me and I knew they were genuinely happy for me. The community support and the continuous encouragement from my brother did a lot to enhance my self-esteem and self-image. I'm very proud to be from Waterbury, Connecticut.

The other quality my brother provides is a sense of calm, a trait that I admire. Perhaps the best example of this took place over twenty-five years ago at Fulton Park, located in the north section of our town. It was a gorgeous day, so my brother and I decided to take the 15-minute walk from our house to the park. My brother was carrying his BB gun and had planned to do some target shooting, a pastime he'd participated in on many occasions with our older cousin at the very same park. When we arrived, we found an isolated area that was away from everyone else. After relaying some basic ground rules to me, my brother went about the business of setting up targets against an old tree. Shortly afterward, we heard sirens. At first, we ignored them. But as the sounds grew closer, we became concerned. Moments later, we found that we were surrounded by police officers with one creeping toward us with a drawn gun. He was telling my brother, in an agitated voice, to "put the gun down!" Larry explained that the weapon was a harmless BB gun that he'd planned to use for his own enjoyment. By this time, I was incensed and yelled out, "Don't shoot my brother, don't shoot my brother." Larry continued to maintain his cool. In a soothing voice, he told me not to worry and he talked to the police officer through each step as he cautiously laid the BB gun on the ground. The officer confiscated the gun, telling my brother that he could pick it up later at the police station. Not surprisingly, my brother never retrieved it. I now realize that my brother's cool demeanor and quick thinking probably saved both our lives. But whenever the story comes up, Larry just feels guilty because he believes he put me in harm's way. In my eyes, however, he will always be my hero and a true father figure.

Speaking of fathers, my father still managed to make an impression even though he wasn't around. He and my mother separated well before my fourth birthday and I rarely saw him over the years. My father was a sick man. As a result of his stint as a soldier in the Korean War, he had gunshot wounds to the head and foot. One of his fingers was shot off. He also experienced flash-backs (Post Traumatic Stress Disorder or PTSD) for many years. Like many war veterans, he slept with his eyes half open and was also an alcoholic. Even in his drunken stupor, my father would still tell us that he loved us.

Despite his erratic behavior, my mother continued to safeguard his reputation, convincing us kids that the man we saw was not the man she knew. "That's not who your father is," she'd say. "He has a disease; he is an alcoholic." Then she'd tell us about the strong man he was and how he was excellent in mathematics. She proudly told us that our dad taught mathematics to foreigners in our melting pot community whose primary language was Italian, Spanish or Polish. According to my mother, much of my father's behavior was due to the stress and untold terror caused by the war. It seemed his secrets from the experience haunted him yet he was unwilling or at least unable to release them. As an example, my brother told me that he and my sister, Tawanda, would ask my father (affectionately known as Big Ernie) if he'd ever killed a man in combat. He never gave them a straight answer and would always change the subject. The only thing Big Ernie would reveal was that he had to go for days without real food, surviving only on grass and water. He also told them repeatedly how much the soldiers had to rely on each other for survival. It was never clear whether my father's evasiveness was to protect us or to protect himself. But whatever the case, his response painted a grim picture for me and war was something that I never wanted to experience. Even at a young age, I realized my father lived a hard life.

Some of my most memorable moments with my father include the times when he took us for rides in the countryside in an attempt to teach my mom how to drive. These excursions gave us kids the opportunity to soak up some new surroundings. Even though the areas where Big Ernie took us were no more than thirty minutes away, it seemed like a lifetime away when we compared those sights to our own environment at home. Our father may not have intended to expand our horizons, but those short trips did just that.

Unfortunately, there isn't much else for me to recall when it comes to my dad. Since my mom never spoke ill of him, I didn't develop a negative perception of him. But his absence prevented us from developing a lasting, true father-and-son relationship. I never got to know him or his family in a way that I would have liked or deserved. He has since passed away. Perhaps the biggest lessons I took from him were ones he never knew he taught me. As I watched his illnesses prevent him from enjoying his life to the fullest, I learned the importance of maintaining good health for a sound mind and body. Most importantly, I learned the power of forgiveness, especially when it comes to those people in our lives who may not realize how much they have failed us.

Our brain operates much like a computer, enabling us to take mental notes, pictures and recordings of situations and people that influenced our lives. By exploring the many memories that we've collected, we're able to use the past to impact our future. I invite you to tap the databank containing your childhood memories so you can use those experiences to help you make some positive changes in your life.

For me, I tap the past to help me overcome some of my own shortcomings. One of the things I do to relax is pray and meditate. Those thoughts force me to keep things in perspective and realize that I can achieve more with a positive attitude than I can with a negative one. By the same token, I think about my mom whenever I face a difficult challenge. According to her, anything good is worth fighting for. So, I think about her whenever I need the inspiration to keep forging ahead. My grandmother's memory also provides me with inspiration from a spiritual sense. She taught us that God would not plant the seed of desire in your heart if that dream were not achievable. So when there are things in life that I want, I know that God placed them there and they are well within my reach, even if I can't quite figure out the details yet.

What is your past trying to communicate to you? Think about the messages that you've received from your childhood and use them wisely. Remember those experiences don't necessarily have to be positive for you take a positive lesson from them. Instead of focusing on my dad's absence, I concentrate on those times when he was around because those were happy times for us. And for those of you who didn't have your father at all, you can at least recall how that made you feel as a child so you avoid making the same mistake.

As the twig is bent, so shall the tree grow. Negative childhood influences can influence behavior. Environmental influences can have an impact on how a child behaves as an adult. As you reconnect with your past, use this opportunity to take an honest assessment. Start by asking yourself four important questions: 1) What family members influenced me the most? 2) What specific events had an effect on me? 3) What lessons did I learn from the people and events that had the greatest effect on me? and 4) How can I apply these lessons learned in my everyday life? Record your answers and put them in a safe place so you can refer to them frequently. Next, determine the things about yourself that you'd like to improve and refer to members of your family for inspiration. Know that the changes you seek may not happen overnight and you might need help for a complete transformation. That's okay. Pray. Talk to someone for clarity or advice, write a letter, or seek counseling: just do it. Do whatever you need to do for healing.

Also, make a promise to yourself: Always focus on the positive in any given situation. Once you've done this, you've already won half the battle. Reading scripture and strengthening your relationship with the Lord will help you maintain a positive perspective, but just understand that it's an ongoing journey. Putting a perpetual positive perspective into play isn't always easy. Many of the people you have in your life are pessimistic by nature because they just don't know any better. They think they're preventing you from getting hurt or they're so used to being negative they don't know anything else. Be a shining example for them. Show your family members a new point of view. Let them know that you don't automatically have to recreate the same patterns that occurred in your childhood, especially if those patterns no longer work for you. Instead, keep the practices that serve you and get rid of the ones that don't. You can change! You just need to be committed to make a change and your willingness to read this book means you're definitely on your way to carving a path for a new beginning. Acknowledging that your family unit is very special and believing that you were placed in that environment for a divine reason is a very important part of the process. These steps enable you to discover another essential component of your true identity. Your education is the element we'll assess next.

UOICE OF EHPERIEMCE #3

Dr. Jeff Carter, an African American, had been a good student. Although he finished medical school, he had difficulty performing well on tests and failed his medical boards twice. Because of his great reputation during his residency, he was hired over two non-Black applicants for a position at a local hospital. The other residents had passed their boards. Dr. Carter struggled with his feelings of guilt and inadequacy. Although he believed in Affirmative Action, he did not like feeling as though he had not earned the opportunity. His feelings of inferiority caused him to overcompensate by being somewhat controlling when dealing with people. Dr. Carter had to explore the residual

*effects of slavery and the Jim Crow era to understand that
we are still working to develop a level playing field. He
was competent, effective, and conscientious in his work.
As he began to excel at the hospital and supervisors
praised him and acknowledged his contributions, he began
to internalize feelings of competency. In fact, it was one
supervisor who challenged him about his behavior that
helped him to see that he did not have to overcompensate.
Although we as Black men frequently believe that we have
to be "twice as good" to be given the same opportunities,
this does not always ring true in every area. Dr. Carter
was twice as good in his performance and work ethic, but
he did not have to prove himself by overachieving.*

EDUCATE YOURSELF ABOUT EDUCATION

Outside of your spirituality and family, your education is one of
the strongest influences on your life. As you continue to embark
down the road to self-discovery, try to understand how your education fits into your overall identity. Now when we look at education, we're not necessarily referring to education in the traditional school system. Sometimes, people with a formal education
are no more intelligent than those who chose to leave the system
before graduating high school. I have friends who have not gone
to college who are as intelligent as I am and I have a Ph.D. Some
have been able to successfully operate small businesses and others have overcome obstacles inherent in impoverished communities and managed to succeed without a formal education. At the
same time, there are benefits to being able to maneuver through
the traditional educational system. Obtaining a formal education,
for example, enables you to participate in society at various levels and in different environments. Your available career choices,
whether they be entry level or managerial, are largely based on
the level of education that you have achieved. This, in some

instances, determines how we're able to financially care for our families and ourselves, and participate in the social and democratic elements of our society. Knowledge is power. Thus, our level of education inspires us to contribute to the betterment of our community and our world.

Black men who are educated make higher salaries than those who are not. In addition, they are less likely to be incarcerated and more likely to be progressive citizens. Beyond that, they serve as examples so that future generations can follow their lead. In my case, education provided me with other avenues of success so I didn't have to emulate the dope dealers in my neighborhood. The more educated I became, the more options I had available to me. Part of our responsibility to this generation is to help our Black males see school as an opportunity rather than an obstacle. To do that, we must first re-evaluate our viewpoints regarding the current educational structure and make the necessary changes in the system that will better enable us to successfully participate.

Everything starts with you. One of the best things you can do to help your community and yourself is lead by example and ensure that charity starts on the home front. Don't just encourage the children in your life to go to school, but show them how it's done by furthering your own education. Besides the fact that you will raise your own earning potential, you'll also inspire those people in your circle who look up to you. Remember, we said that adults are simply replaying many of the same scripts that they learned when they were children. The same is true here. If the children in your environment see the importance you place on education, that knowledge will travel with them as well. They'll be lugging their books to class right along with you.

But let's not stop there. Start working the system instead of allowing the system to work you. As strong Black males, we need to make things happen instead of allowing things to happen to us. Most of us just ended up going to our zone schools and subject our children to the same plight. Why is that? Other communities seek out the best and get it. We're very much a part of the American system and we've earned and deserve the same benefits and opportunities that our white counterparts enjoy on a daily basis. There is a long list of free specialized public educational programs that are available but it's up to us to take full advantage of them. Whether you or your child is an underachiever or an overachiever, there are government-funded programs specifically designed to help you both excel. Let's seek out these opportunities by visiting various schools and the district office in your area. Also, develop relationships with school counselors and teachers, surf the Net, go to the library and bookstores, and show a true interest in the opportunities that are available. Before you know it, you'll have access to more information than you could have ever imagined. The Bible tells us to knock and it shall be given to you and seek and you shall find. It really is that simple.

It's also up to us, Black people, to discover new and exciting ways to design and participate in an educational system so that it truly supports Black people. A push for culturally-based learning and teaching strategies has emerged in several neighborhoods so that Black students can learn about significant Black people in history. Black students can also participate in African dance, write lyrics for rap music, and see powerful visual imagery as they study their subjects.

Mentorship programs are also designed to provide Black students with positive role models for success, as are schools that look to hire more African American teachers. Smaller schools with fewer students in the classroom can make a difference and so can schools that choose to expand their curriculum to include nontraditional subjects that deal with conflict resolution, anger management, meditation, drug abuse prevention, psychological counseling, and interpersonal skills training. If you think these programs will benefit the educational institutions in your area, speak up. Meanwhile, start your own mentoring program by simply connecting with some of the youth in your community.

Education is a key part of your identity. But it's not only about what you've learned during the course of your life, but what information you've passed on to your community, and how you use what you've learned to create a brighter future.

VOICE OF EXPERIENCE #4

Billy currently attends a predominately white university. In his first year of college, he had trouble fitting in. Many of the African American students were from blue collar or low-income homes. Since Billy came from a predominately white, middle-class environment, he felt he just couldn't relate to them. In an effort to resolve the issue, he decided to become more active in the Black Student Union (BSU). But when Billy attended the meetings, the other students simply made fun, accusing him of dressing and acting like a white boy. As a result, Billy stopped attending BSU meetings and started befriending some of the white students. However, he wasn't entirely comfortable with that either. Then one day, he decided to discuss his challenges with his father.

"Growing up in poverty is not a prerequisite to being Black," his father explained. According to Billy's dad, his parents would have chosen an all-Black neighborhood over the white one where they lived, but they couldn't find one that afforded the types of resources that they currently had available. "We moved for better opportunities," he clarified, not because they didn't want to associate with other Blacks. As a suggestion, he told Billy to learn as much as he could from other Black students while teaching them about his environment. "Be strong and fearless!"

Billy's father ordered. "Believe that in your spirit and be proud of who you are."

That was all the motivation Billy needed to return to BSU and declare his rightful place among his brothers and sisters. Initially, the students acted much as they had before, making fun of Billy's clothes and speech. But this time, Billy wasn't defeated by those comments. Instead, he became revitalized. "All of us have unique experiences that we can share with each other and we all have challenges as Black people," he announced. "Instead of focusing on our differences, let's look at how much we can benefit from each other." And with that statement, he instantly struck a chord with his classmates. Soon Billy was hanging out with BSU members outside of scheduled meetings. In fact, he'd become so popular in his junior year that he was elected president. When asked why she voted for Billy, one student delightfully responded, "He may talk funny, but he's done a lot to help the Black Student Union organization. That's why I voted for him."

Like Billy, your Blackness can be the key to new and exciting opportunities. As illustrated in the above anecdote, knowing that you have value, being fearless, willingly learning about others, and committing to sharing your own knowledge with the people in your community can have phenomenal results. And that's exactly why you're reading this book—to transform yourself into the best Black male that God has intended.

There are no limits to your greatness. You are the chosen one. And like a strong oak tree, your roots run deep. And those connections will provide you with everything that you need to achieve and enjoy your personal best.

Billy's story also tells us the importance of knowing who you are. Once Billy discovered himself as a Black male, he was able to appreciate the value in others and in himself. The same thing is true for you. Before you take that first step toward growing strong and powerful, you need to know who you are. You need to be crystal clear about your identity. For our purposes, your identity is your life's seed. It is the foundation you need for building a better future.

DRAFT YOUR DREAM TEAM

You've heard the saying that it's not what you know but who you know. My question to you is: Who do you know? By now, you should have taken time out in your life to cultivate relationships that really matter. But whether you've developed such bonds, your social ties are part of your identity. The social connections you make should be with people you know have your back. These people should be enthusiastic, positive, successful Christian men. Choose your friends the way you would pick who you would want on your basketball team. You want strong, determined, supportive men who can handle the ball and deal with pressure. Surround yourself with brothers who are genuinely on your team.

From the very beginning, it's clear that God created us to be a part of a community. The Bible tells us that in the Garden of Eden. God said, "It is not good for man to be alone." From birth, we are born as members of the human race and once we join God's family, we become members of the body of Christ. In every aspect of our existence, it seems that we need to interact with other people to fulfill our true purpose. Just think, if an organ is cut from your body, it will surely die. The same is true for you. Your social connections serve as your own life source.

Most importantly, you need to connect with God. As stated earlier, this relationship is the most important factor of your identity because it clarifies to you and others to whom you belong. It provides you with a spiritual covering that will keep you safe and help you excel in all areas of your life. At the same time, the way to further strengthen this relationship is to connect with people who have the same beliefs that you do. A great way to ensure this is to find a church in your area that aligns with your beliefs and values. Joining a church will make you accountable to yourself and the people you begin to socialize with, provide you with opportunities to demonstrate your faith, and strengthen your commitment to your beliefs. As long as you practice your beliefs in isolation, the validity of those beliefs can never truly be tested. Beyond that, fellowship allows you to support others and enables others to support you through life's daily challenges. In *The Purpose Driven Life: What on earth am I here for?* (Zondervan, 2002) by Rick Warren, the author says that, "attendees are consumers; members are contributors." But here's the thing: Members get more benefits than attendees even though they're the ones primarily doing the giving. Try it and see.

Now, I know that Black men are usually a minority when it comes to church. That's okay. Your presence there will help to attract others and serve as proof that there are Black men who are publicly willing to show their commitment to God. As the Bible says, if you stand up for God, He will stand up for you. But don't just attend as a spectator, get involved. Contribute your talents for the betterment of the church and God's purpose and you'll receive more blessings than you can ever imagine. Churches are seeking strong men who have struggled and can give testimony about it. Pastors would welcome you, and you will provide inspiration to others.

This habit of connecting with people that share your beliefs is not something that you'd just do from a spiritual perspective. Do this in every aspect of your life because your destiny is tied to those people with whom you are affiliated. Only have relationships with people who are headed in the same direction that you want to go. Otherwise, you'll suffer the same fate that they will simply because of your association.

There are other things you need to know to socialize successfully. Relationships require a certain amount of reciprocity. Between the people involved, everyone gets a chance to give and everyone receives at some point. The participants depend on each other and should be honest with one another. The people involved should be considerate and respect each other's differences. Strive to meet the people who are in your social circle on some type of regular basis. How often have we waited months or even years to reconnect with someone we consider a dear friend only to realize that the relationship has changed over time? It's not the same as we left it and it shouldn't be, because relationships take work and you have to be willing to invest in them if you want them to grow. In addition, there needs to be a certain amount of vulnerability involved. That means that you and the other members need to feel free to express failures, hurts, doubts, fears, weaknesses or limitations without the fear of betrayal. At the same time, the degree of openness should be related to the level of trust involved in the relationship. So, it wouldn't benefit you or be fair to the other person if you started revealing extremely personal things to someone whom you barely know or to someone who had already proven himself to be untrustworthy. Often times we become disappointed by people who have violated our trust and then we shut down to everyone else in the future. But if we had really looked at the person to whom we chose to reveal ourselves, we would have known better.

Improving our social circle also requires that we start becoming one of the people that we hope to surround ourselves with. If we want trustworthy, honest, friendly, strong, motivated, approachable, and loving people in our lives, for instance, we need to ask ourselves if we are those things. If we're not, we should implement a plan for self-development. The benefits of having strong, loving, long-lasting relationships far outweigh the effort it takes to cultivate them. Start making those critical connections today.

BIG WHITE LIES

It's time that we break free of anything that could potentially hold us in physical or mental bondage. Although there are racists who still want to hold onto lies about the Black male and his role in the universe, we know that Black men are leaders, conquerors, intellectuals, and lovers by design. Instead of focusing on the untruths that society tries to perpetuate about Black men, focus on what God has to say about you at the end of the chapter.

How are you going to start making things happen? You've already got the tools. As the saying goes, if God is for you, who can be against you? Nobody. So feel liberated because you now know that whatever limitations people have put on you are nothing but lies. As long as you declare that you are a child of the King of Kings, your attitude is the only thing that stands between yourself and your goals. Your attitude can be your biggest help on your journey to success. By internalizing this one lesson alone, you can change your life and the lives of the people around you. This renewed perspective will empower you and others to realize the power that comes with relying on and believing in God.

Despite what you've been taught to believe in the past, it really doesn't matter what others say about you. The real question is, how do you see yourself and what resources you are relying on to reach those conclusions? Joel Osteen, author of *Your Best Life Now: 7 steps to living at your full potential* (Warner, 2004), points out that your biggest battle is in your mind. "You will never go beyond the barriers in your own mind. If you think you can't do something, then you never will. The battle is in your mind. If you are defeated in your mind, you've already lost the battle. If you don't think your dreams will ever come to pass, they never will. If you don't think you have what it takes to rise up and set that new standard, it's not going to happen." Start making things happen.

Society's effect on you is the last component that determines your identity. The good news here is that you have the power to redefine that as you continue to walk in God's light. The closer you get to God, the more you realize just how little society's perceptions matter.

PLANT THE SEED

Now that you've been introduced to all of the elements that make up your identity, you are ready to plant the seed. Select ground that has been fertilized with your self-love and the love of Jesus Christ. Then, plant all of the elements you need: a strong relationship with the Holy Spirit, all of the positive practices that you learned from your family, the knowledge that you obtained from your educational system, the strong social ties with your dream team that will help facilitate change and your renewed world view to ensure growth. Your tree will grow taller than you can ever imagine.

In Chapter I, we attempt to eliminate any confusion you may have had about who you are by taking a close look at your identity. The scriptures below tell you exactly what God has to say about you. Refer to this list for inspiration and guidance.

WHO I AM IN CHRIST?

I am God's child for I am born again of the incorruptible seed of the Word of God which lives and abides forever *(I Peter 1:21)*

I am forgiven of all my sins and washed in the blood *(Eph. 1:3; Heb. 9:14; Col. 1:14; 1 John 2:12; 1 John 1:9)*

I am a new creation *(II Cor. 5:17)*

I am a temple where the Holy Spirit lives *(I Cor. 6:19)*

I am delivered from the power of darkness and Christ brings me into God's kingdom *(Col. 1:13)*

I am redeemed from the curse of the law *(I Pet. 1:18)*

I am blessed *(Deut. 28:1-14; Gal. 3:9)*

I am a saint *(Rom. 1:7; I Cor. I:2; Phil. 1:1)*

I am holy and without blame before Him in love *(Eph. 2:13)*

I am established to the end *(I Cor. 1:8)*

I have been brought closer to God through the blood of Christ *(Eph. 2:13)*

I am victorious *(Rev. 21:7)*

I am set free *(John 8:31-33)*

I am strong in the Lord *(Eph. 6:20)*

I am dead to sin *(Rom. 6:2, 11; I Pet. 2:24)*

I am more than a conqueror *(Rom. 3:37)*

I am a co-heir with Christ *(Rom. 8:17)*

I am sealed with the Holy Spirit of Promise *(Eph. 1:13)*

I am in Christ Jesus by His doing *(I Cor. 1:30)*

I am accepted in Jesus Christ *(Eph. 1:6)*

I am complete in Him *(Col. 2:10)*

I am crucified with Christ *(Gal. 2:20)*

I am alive with Christ *(Eph. 2:5)*

I am free from condemnation *(Rom. 8:1)*

I am reconciled of God *(II Cor. 5:18)*

I am qualified to share in His inheritance *(Col. 1:12)*

I am firmly rooted, established in my faith and overflowing with gratefulness/thankfulness *(Col. 2:7)*

I am a fellow citizen with the saints and of the household of God *(Eph. 2:19)*

I am built upon the foundation of the apostles and prophets, Jesus Christ Himself being the Chief Cornerstone *(Eph. 2:20)*

I am in the world as He is in Heaven *(1 John 4:17)*

I am born of God and the evil one does not touch me *(1 John 5:18)*

I am His faithful follower *(Rev. 17:14)*

I am overtaken with blessings *(Deut. 28:2; Eph. 1:3)*

I am His disciple because I have love for others *(John 13:34, 35)*

I am the light of the world *(Matt. 5:14)*

I am the salt of the earth *(Matt. 5:13)*

I am the righteousness of God *(II Cor. 5:21; I Pet 2:24)*

I am a partaker of His divine nature *(II Pet. 1:4)*

I am called of God *(II Tim. 1:9)*

I am chosen *(I Thess. 1:4; Eph. 1:4, I Pet. 2:9)*

I am an ambassador of Christ *(II Cor. 5:20)*

I am God's workmanship created in Christ Jesus for good works *(Eph. 2:10)*

I am the apple of my Father's eye *(Deut 32:10; Ps. 17:8)*

I am healed by the stripes of Jesus *(I Pet. 2:24; Is. 53:6)*

I am being changed into His image *(II Cor. 3:18; Phil. 1:6)*

I am raised up with Christ and am seated in heavenly places *(Col. 2:12; Eph. 2:6)*

I am beloved of God *(Col. 3:12; Rom. 1:7; 1 Thess. 1:4)*

I am one in Christ! Hallelujah! *(John 17:21-23)*

I have the mind of Christ *(Phil. 2:5; I Cor. 2:16)*

I have obtained an inheritance *(Eph. 1:11)*

I have access by one Spirit to the Father *(Eph. 2:18)*

I have overcome the world *(I John 5:4)*

I have everlasting life and will not be condemned *(John 5:24; John 6:47)*

I have the peace of God which transcends all understanding *(Phil. 4:7)*

I have received power, the power of the Holy Spirit; power to lay hands on the sick and see them recover; power to chase out demons; power over all the power of the enemy and nothing shall be any means to hurt me. *(Mark 16:17, 18; Mark 10; 17-19)*

I live by and in the law of the spirit of life in Christ Jesus *(Rom. 8-2)*

I walk in Christ Jesus *(Col. 2:6)*

I can do all things (everything) in and through Christ Jesus *(Rom. 8:2)*

I possess the Greater one in me because greater is He who is in me than he who is in the world *(I John 4:4)*

I press toward the mark for the prize of the high calling in God *(Phil. 3:14)*

I always triumph in Christ *(II Cor. 2:14)*

I show forth His praise in my life *(I Pet. 2:9)*

I died and my life is now hidden with Christ in God *(Col. 3:3)*

— **Compiled by James Perry, Ph.D.**
Light of the World Training Center

CHAPTER TWO

·≪≋≋≋≫·

Fertilizing the Soil:
Love Thy Self

FERTILIZING THE SOIL: ASSESSMENT STATEMENTS

Not at all				**Very much**
1	2	3	4	5

1. I love myself.

2. I do things to demonstrate that I love myself.

3. I engage in self-destructive behavior.

4. I know I'm God's special child.

5. I am gifted and talented.

FERTILIZING THE SOIL: PERSONAL INVENTORY

1. I recite the following positive affirmations:

2. I love myself because:

3. I feel good about my accomplishments in:

4. God loves me because:

5. My special gifts and talents are:

NOTE: You will find inventory questions throughout this book. Please take advantage of the space left open to you to jot down your own notes and personal thoughts as you move through the text. You may find it helpful to review your notes from time to time to assess your progress or revisit an idea at a later date.

APPLAUSE

I believe we all yearn in some child-like way,
To dazzle in the spotlight at front and center stage.
To one day speak from the grand podium,
While listening eyes rave and never once stray.

Applause, like an old song or cornered souvenir,
The memory embeds, the very moment we hear.
For that duration of acceptance is our time in a bottle,
We bask in the happening and reflect tomorrow.

It is high and never low, it is found and never lost,
When coming from the heart, it will surely cost.
For a tear will start to glisten, you have truly been touched,
A timely pat on one's back is never too much.

We will always need to hear the wonderful sound
Of applause.

— **Larry Toussaint Garlington**

KNOWING GOD'S UNCONDITIONAL LOVE

Do you feel that the best thing about you is you? You don't base your feelings about yourself on your position at work, your romantic relationship, or your role in the community. Understand your true value is intrinsic, not extrinsic. Value yourself, love yourself, and don't equate your self-worth with what you do or what people say about you. As a child of God, you are primarily concerned about what He has to say about you. Beyond that, understand that the creator and his creations are wonderful and marvelous. And since you are His creation, you are also wonderful and marvelous. You can't let situations get you down because you have a strong sense of self-worth and self-love.

But what is love exactly? True love for another person is an appreciation for who that person is. The same goes for you. When you love yourself, you accept yourself fully, the good and the "need to improve" portion of yourself. Contrary to many romantic notions that you've traditionally heard, true love is not blind. When someone loves someone or something blindly, they don't know what they actually love. Love is extremely knowledgeable. To love yourself is to know yourself and you do that by intimately connecting with God and your own thoughts.

Closely examine your actions, behaviors, and insights from an objective point of view and appreciate them. Think about how you responded to certain situations. Did you make the best decision based on the information that you had available? If so, don't look back. Instead, move on. If you think you could have done better, vow to do better next time. Accept your flaws, even if it means you have to laugh or cry in response to them. The important thing is that you continue loving yourself at whatever point you are in your development. In loving yourself, you understand that your life is a journey that requires that you continuously move forward to becoming better, more righteous, and more spiritually connected.

It's easy to love when things are good and the people in our lives are good to us. However, continue to love when you feel like the world is against you and you are the last person standing. Love takes courage. But you can love in barren times and in times of harvest as long as you believe in your heart that what you're doing is right and you're not hurting anyone. The Bible even requires that we love our enemy, illustrating that if we can love someone who doesn't love us, then loving ourselves under any condition should be easy, especially since God continues to love us unconditionally.

God loves you more than any other person in the world. In fact, God loves you more than anyone else is capable of loving of you. That's what makes Him God. He can love each and every one of us as uniquely as if we were the only person on Earth. To feel and understand His unconditional and unfailing love for us is awesome. It is difficult for us to love something completely through our tainted eyes or through the eyes of other people. But, if we look through God's perfect eyes, then we know that we can love perfectly because we are a perfect creation through Him. When you think about how special you are through the eyes of the Lord, you can truly, truly, believe that you are great and worthy of that unconditional love.

God's love has nothing to do with your behavior. God doesn't love us for the things that we do; He loves us because of who we are. Just think about how much you truly love your children. Your love for them isn't really based on what they say or do, particularly when they are infants. You're not focused on their shortcomings but looking for ways to make them better. That's just how God feels about us. His love for us is exponentially deeper than your love for your own children. Imagine that.

There's another way that you know God loves you. He allows situations to come into your life to test you. It's only through those tests that your true character is developed and revealed to you. You are always being tested. Life is a test. God is constantly observing your responses to people, circumstances, triumphs, tragedies, surprises and disappointments to assess how much you've grown from the last incident. And the situations don't always have to be grand. Think about how you reacted when someone cut you off while you were driving to work. Or, recall how you reacted to the waiter when he mixed up your order. Or maybe you thought someone disrespected you. Did you do the same thing to him or her?

There are also times when we are faced with major changes in our lives and God stands by to see how we handle them. Sometimes, we don't feel His closeness, but we know that since God never leaves us, He is never far away, even when we don't feel His presence. All of these occurrences are things that God uses to shape and mold us. Most importantly, God takes the time to invest in us because of His love for us.

VOICE OF EXPERIENCE #5

Hakeem and Jason grew up together and played football on their high school's state championship team. Jason, the number-one rated quarterback in the state, was heavily recruited by the Division 1 teams in the country. Hakeem was the leading rusher in the state and was recruited heavily by 1AA teams. They were both offered full scholarships to separate colleges and maintained contact during their college careers. Both of them won starting positions on their teams and became college superstars. Hakeem led the nation in rushing, while Jason's team was ranked num-

*ber seven in the country and he was the starting quarter-
back. To outsiders, both of the young men lived lives that
most people only realized in their dreams.*

*Though Jason enjoyed much more national attention than
Hakeem, he also felt an overwhelming amount of pressure
to perform. During mid-season, Jason lost a big game and
became depressed. Hakeem tried to encourage him.
"You'll get 'em next time," he insisted, but Jason couldn't
get over the disappointment expressed by his teammates
and it made him feel like a failure.*

*Months later, Hakeem tore his ACL and the knee injury set
him back. Though he received treatment for it, he was
never able to fully recover. His football career came to a
swift end. Ironically, Jason also experienced a dramatic
setback. After his fourth concussion of his career, his doctor recommended that he stop playing football. The two
men tried to console each other, but Jason was deeply
wounded and felt like he was nothing without football.
"You think that you were great because of your football
career?" Hakeem quizzed after participating in a long, difficult conversation. "If that's the case, you're wrong; you
are great with or without football."*

*Although he felt sorry for his friend, Hakeem decided that
he would use the same energy that he used for football
and direct it toward his academics and community service.
Even though he never suited up in a football jersey again,
he remained a star player, being recognized for his out-
standing achievements in his studies and in his community.
"I was good at football because I tried to focus on being a
great man," he said in a speech he delivered at his college
graduation. "That way, when my football career went by
the wayside, I was still left with the best part me — my
mind!"*

LOVING YOURSELF FULLY

Loving yourself is an action. It requires that you actually do things to demonstrate love. Think about the things you do to demonstrate your self-love: How do you treat yourself? What do you say about yourself? What do you think about yourself? What messages do you communicate about yourself to others (either by what you say or your behavior)? What expectations do you have of yourself?

Your relationship with the Lord can help you seek a deeper understanding of yourself and help you find ways to demonstrate your self-love. This is a wonderful way to transform your aggression into a more positive life force. Plan fun and joyful things. Do positive self-affirming activities. Recite affirmations in the mirror such as, "I am the man, I can't be stopped, and I'm looking good." Don't commit to things you'd rather not do. Allow yourself the luxury and pleasure of something nice on occasion. Treat yourself.

One of the things you can do to actively love yourself is to get into the practice of positive self-talk. Use affirmations such as, "I love myself and I care about myself," "I am a good positive person," and "I am an achiever." Set up a daily routine. You need to have an internal mechanism so that if someone were to open you up inside, they would be warmed by your internal sunshine. If you don't feel this way now, then ask yourself: "What is inside of me?"

Only you know the deepest part of you, but the way you act and the way you treat people is a strong indication of how you feel about yourself. Ask yourself some questions: What is my emotional state? Do I typically walk in happiness regardless of the circumstances? When I am down, do I have mechanisms to improve my mood? Do I know what things provide me with lasting joy? Do I have my own standards of accomplishments or do I rely on others for encouragement? Finding answers to these questions is critical to actively loving yourself.

Develop a daily routine that includes taking time out of your schedule to actively love yourself. Maintain an upbeat attitude and if you're not feeling great, do something healthy to boost your mood. If you have a long-term problem, such as depression, find specific ways to resolve these issues (we'll talk about this more later on). Get in the habit of putting yourself and your feelings first. Other than God, be number one in your life. Learning how to actively love yourself is essential to cultivating positive relationships. Although it's a cliché, you really can't love anyone else until you fully love yourself.

EXPRESSING LOVE TO OTHERS

Believe it or not, the tongue is one of God's greatest gifts to us because whatever we say, we can create. That's why it's important that we use our tongue to express our love to one another and ourselves. Instead of focusing on the negative, promote the positive. A lot of us grew up only hearing negative things about Black people.

For instance, I grew up in a neighborhood where we would spend hours just putting each other down. We literally attacked each other. We insulted everything from families to our friends to our appearances. Whatever were the lowest things that could be said about another person, we said it. It has been called ranking, cracking, playing the dozens. Supposedly, it was all in fun, but those comments hurt. I know people felt pain when they went home because I felt pain. It also hurt me to say such negative things about my friends. From that experience, I learned to make a conscious decision to say positive things about other people, especially fellow Black males and genuinely mean them.

Make a conscious decision to say positive things to another Black man and express them in a way that would show why you respect him. Get to know their spirit and appreciate them. Then choose words and expressions that build them up, not defeat them. Your expressions of brotherly love promote greater trust between you and other Black men. This positive step will help you build stronger relationships that will serve you well throughout the course of your life. Remember, as Black men, we're in battle to protect our community and reclaim the inheritance that is rightfully ours. When you're at war, you need people by your side that you care about and can trust. You can only achieve this by being willing to express love to your brother.

TAKING GOOD CARE OF YOU

Unlike your car, your body doesn't come with a warranty. This is the only body you have and it's nearly impossible to get replacement parts. As much as you'd like to, you can't take your body to the junkyard and request another one. And just like your car, regular maintenance is a much more efficient approach than making repairs in the midst of an emergency. It seems like an obvious observation when the discussion is focused on cars, but it's time you apply this rationale to yourself as well.

Proper maintenance is essential if you want to ensure that you stay in working order. Plus, your willingness to get regular checkups is the best way you can show love for yourself and love for the people who care about you. By taking good care of yourself, you save the people in your life a lot of unnecessary anguish, worry, and suffering. Beyond that, you stand as an example to other men who need some extra motivation to take that first step toward better health. Here are some things that you can start doing today to better manage your health:

- **EAT HEALTHY.** The saying, "You are what you eat," is so true. Doing simple things can make a world of difference. Start by cutting down on your red meat intake (reduce the amount of red meat you eat to the size of a deck of cards per week); increasing your vegetables, fruits and salads (have at least five different colored vegetables in your salad minus the fatty dressing); cutting out the dairy; consuming more whole grains (breads, rice and cereal); and reducing the amount of carbohydrates you eat. Eliminate fatty foods from your diet because they increase your risk of prostate cancer and contribute to other health problems. Vary your menu by including things such as fruit smoothies, fruit kabobs and veggie omelets. According to the National Cancer Institute, an organization encouraging Black men to eat at least five to nine servings of vegetables and fruits daily, dietary changes may reduce the risk of certain diseases that disproportionately affect African American men. In short, the more fruits and vegetables you add to your life, the more years you have ahead of you.

- **DRINK EIGHT TO TEN GLASSES OF WATER A DAY.** This alone will help clear the toxins out of your system and keep your skin healthier so you look years younger.

- **EXERCISE.** You can make a big difference in your overall health by exercising for only one hour, three days out of the week. And we're not talking about major physical work. You can get your heart pumping by doing activities such as skiing, walking, dancing, jogging, running, swimming, doing TaeBo or shooting some hoops with the fellas. All you have to do is ensure that the hours you spend exercising contain twenty minutes of continuous exercise on alternate days. And you will reap the benefits, which also include a boost in self-esteem, more relaxation, lower anxiety and better sleep. Exercise is really a must for longevity and there are certain conditions (such as diabetes, high cholesterol and heart disease) that require some degree of exercise for management. Just get a clean bill of health from your doctor before you tackle any physical activity, incorporate a good "warmup" and "cool down" in your exercise routine, get an exercise buddy for motivation, and be consistent.

• **KNOW THAT PREVENTION IS THE BEST CURE.** As stated earlier, get regular checkups to fend off medical conditions or at least get early treatments if you find out you have a negative diagnosis.

• **ASK QUESTIONS.** When you visit your doctor's office, don't just sit there; ask questions. Find out as much information as you can about your health. If you have symptoms that you're concerned about, let your doctor know. Make sure you get copies of your own medical records, test results, and doctor's commentary. If there is anything in your records that you don't understand, get clarification. Change your doctor if you don't feel comfortable with him or her.

• **GET TESTED.** Whether you think you may have been exposed to HIV or any STD, or have another condition such as prostrate or testicular cancer or diabetes, ask your healthcare provider to test you for these illnesses to determine your status. In regard to prostrate cancer, for example, the American Cancer Society suggests that Black men ages 45 and older be tested annually. If it turns out you have a medical condition, seek early treatment and follow the doctor's orders.

- **BE IN THE KNOW.** Educate yourself about health issues that affect Black men. Talk to other family members to get a more complete medical history. Attend conferences, health fairs, and seminars on African American health. Search the Internet for information. Also, contact organizations such as the American Diabetes Association's African American Program (800-DIA-BETES) or the American Cancer Society (800-227-2345) for additional insight.

- **SPREAD THE WORD.** Don't keep this information to yourself. Let the other men in your life—your father, grandfathers, sons, friends, uncles and colleagues—know the importance of maintaining a healthy lifestyle.

GETTING THE HELP YOU NEED

So far, everything we've talked about has been under your control. But dealing with some of the issues that challenge your mental health are things that you can't necessarily deal with on your own. Sometimes you might need the help of a close friend or confidant. Other times you might need the expertise of a Christian counselor, psychologist, psychiatrist, therapist or other mental health professional. Whatever the case, get the help you need as soon as you can to break free of the things that keep your mind in bondage.

If you are having a particular challenge with self-love and loving others, consider working with a professional to determine if you need treatment. Don't ever think seeking professional help is a weakness because your willingness to move toward self-improvement is a big strength. Read the descriptions below and determine if any of them sound familiar to you. Even if they don't, consider seeing a counselor if you just want to talk about your personal issues. Here are some challenges that may be troubling you and some things you can do for healing.

HANDLING DEPRESSION, ANXIETY, PTSD, ETC.

The Diagnosis and Statistical Manual (DSMIV) provides understanding of symptoms, diagnosis and treatment. The following are the most prevalent conditions among Black men:

DEPRESSIVE DISORDERS OR DYSTHYMIC DISORDERS. These conditions are characterized by intense feelings of sadness, loss, hopelessness, rejection and failure. They range in severity from dysthymic disorders being the least severe to clinical or major depression being the most severe.

Although suicide has been the third-leading cause of death among African American males between ages 15-24 since 1980, many of us remain in denial about depression. We simply don't see it as a problem in the Black community and many therapists say few Black men are willing to talk about the issue at all. But this problem is too big to ignore. Myths surrounding depression and suicide in the Black community are being dispelled by books such as *Standing in the Shadows: Understanding and Overcoming Depression in Black Men* (Broadway, $22.95), by veteran journalist John Head, and *Lay My Burden Down*, co-authored by Dr. Alvin Poussaint, professor of psychiatry at Harvard Medical School. It's also up to each of us to look for the signs of depression in ourselves and the people in our lives.

• **SYMPTOMS**: People who suffer from depression may experience poor appetite or overeating, depressed mood, insomnia or hypersomnia, low energy or fatigue, low self-esteem, poor concentration or difficulty making decisions, feelings of hopelessness or worthlessness, diminished interest or pleasure in activities, or unexpected weight loss or gain. In extreme cases of major depression, there may be recurrent thoughts of death or suicide.

• **TREATMENT**: Individual therapy, group therapy, and participation in enjoyable activities are interventions that help improve mood and functioning. Sometimes antidepressant medication is prescribed.

BIPOLAR DISORDER, *also known as* **MANIC DEPRESSIVE ILLNESS,** is a condition where there is a severe shift in a person's energy, mood, and ability to function. The shift occurs when depression moves from hypomania, where there is a distinct period of elevated, expansive, or irritable mood. This may involve inflated self-esteem or grandiosity, decreased sleep, flights of ideas and excessive involvement in pleasurable activities. It's different from normal ups and downs that everyone experiences.

• **SYMPTOMS**: People with bipolar disorder have dramatic mood swings that range from big "highs" to overwhelming feelings of sadness and hopelessness. Often, energy levels shift dramatically, accompanying the change in mood. These periods of highs and lows are referred to as episodes of depression and mania.

- *TREATMENT*: Sufferers of bipolar disorders can stabilize their mood swings over time with psychosocial treatment and medication.

ANXIETY DISORDER involves excessive worry. This condition can result in restlessness, excessive apprehension, feeling keyed up or on the edge. The person suffering from the condition is easily fatigued and irritable and has difficulty in concentrating. There are five major categories of anxiety disorders, including obsessive-compulsive disorder, panic disorder, social phobia (also known as social anxiety disorder), post traumatic stress disorder, and generalized anxiety disorder.

Anxiety is a normal reaction to stress and can even be a motivator in tense environments such as school, work, or other uncomfortable situations. Generally, anxiety is a mechanism our body uses to cope but when anxiety becomes disabling and affects our ability to deal with everyday life, it requires treatment.

- *SYMPTOMS*: People with this condition may have panic attacks, with palpitations, pounding heart or accelerated heart rate, trembling or shaking, and feelings of choking. Some types of phobias include agoraphobia, where there is fear of going out, and social phobia or fear and avoidance of social situations.

- *TREATMENT*: Psychotherapy, medication and relaxation therapy. Contact your local mental health facility for a referral or treatment options. Also, ask the National Institute of Mental Health (NIMH) if you can participate in the clinical trials for your specific condition.

POST TRAUMATIC STRESS DISORDER is when a person has been exposed to a traumatic event that caused intense fear. The condition may involve recurrent and intrusive recollections of the trauma including images, thoughts, or perceptions. The events that may result in this illness include military combat, natural or human disasters, accidents, or violent personal assaults.

- **SYMPTOMS**: The person with the condition may experience sleep problems, bad dreams, frightening thoughts, illusions or flashbacks, and may avoid anything that could be associated with the trauma. The individual is often easily startled.

- **TREATMENT**: Some people benefit from reliving the experience in a safe and supportive environment. Systematic desensitization where the person gradually learns to face the situation may also be used. Thought stopping and redirection are other alternatives to support the person in coping with trauma.

SOMATIZATION DISORDER is a chronic condition where the patient has numerous physical complaints lasting for years that appear to be psychological in nature because no physical problem has been identified. Typically, the patient complains of pain or problems with the head, abdomen, back, joints, extremities, or chest. The criterion includes pain in four of these areas, two gastrointestinal symptoms, and one sexual symptom, such as severe menstrual cramps or premature ejaculation with pain. The condition can result in substantial impairment as frustrated patients deal with doctors who tell them their complaints are "in your head."

Patients with this condition are often put on medication, even though the physician can find no underlying cause for the physical complaint. Further, symptoms can become so severe that they interfere with the patient's work and personal life. Also symptoms may become worse in times of stress.

• **SYMPTOMS**: The symptoms associated with the condition may depend on the patient's complaint. However, some of the signs of this disorder include abdominal pain, nausea, diarrhea, back pain, joint pain, pain in legs or arm, pain during urination, chest pain, palpitations, dizziness, amnesia, difficulty swallowing, changes in vision, sexual apathy, impotence, and pain during intercourse. Since the symptoms can be associated with actual illnesses, it's important that you receive a thorough physical exam and psychological assessment to rule out other possible medical causes before you receive treatment for somatization disorder.

• **TREATMENT**: If other causes of the symptoms have been ruled out, the patient can receive treatment to help him control the symptoms. In addition, the therapist attempts to uncover underlying mood disorders and individuals may respond to treatments such as antidepressant medication.

INTERMITTENT EXPLOSIVE DISORDER (IED) is associated with violent outbursts of rage, called anger attacks, episodic dyscontrol, or rage attacks. The degree of aggressiveness that the individual expresses during the episodes is grossly out of proportion to the psychological or social stress that he is dealing with. The uncontrolled, unprovoked behavior is not associated with a medical condition or any drug use and has resulted in several instances of destruction of property or physical injury to another person. The condition falls under one of several impulse-control disorders that include pyromania (setting fires), kleptomania (impulsive stealing), or pathological gambling.

- **SYMPTOMS**: The condition is characterized by violent or destructive behavior that has often been present since childhood. A psychologist or psychiatrist, according to results from psychological testing and interviews, diagnoses IED.

- **TREATMENT**: IED is typically treated with some type of drug therapy and psychological treatment to inspire behavior modification. Patients have had good results from mood stabilizers and certain antidepressants.

PERSONALITY DISORDERS are difficult to self-diagnose. Frequently, other people, especially close friends and relatives, see the symptoms and attempt to talk to the person about it but the individual is in denial. Some examples are:

Paranoia — The person has a pattern of pervasive distrust and suspiciousness of others, feels exploited, reads demeaning or threatening meaning into remarks.

Antisocial — Pervasive pattern of disregard for and violation of the rights of others, failure to conform to social norms, deceitfulness, aggressiveness, and reckless disregard for others.

Borderline — Pervasive pattern of instability of interpersonal relationships, self-image and emotions, marked impulsivity and chronic feelings of emptiness.

Narcissistic — Pervasive pattern of grandiosity, need for admiration, lack of empathy and preoccupation with fantasies of unlimited success, power, brilliance, entitlement.

Dependent — Pervasive and excessive need to be taken care of that leads to submissive and clinging behavior and fear of separation.

TRANSFORMING FROM THE INSIDE OUT

An interesting thing happens when you make a decision to love yourself: You actually start doing it. Our minds are so powerful that once we commit to doing something, the universe catches up to our thoughts. If you don't know how to begin your transformation, start simply by seeing yourself as God sees you. He says you are a winner, overcomer, conqueror, champion, and a child of the King. How could you not love yourself? You're God's perfect creation and you were created with a unique purpose.

I MAY BE AT RISK FOR DEVELOPING DEPRESSION

Even though depression is very common, people rarely discuss the condition with their physicians. But, it's important that you do just that if you want to feel better about yourself. If you've answered "Yes" to any of the following questions, you may be depressed and should seek professional advice.

1. Have you consistently been in a bad or down mood for most of the day for at least two weeks?

    Yes   *No*

2. Have you been getting less enjoyment from your usual activities?

    Yes   *No*

3. Have you recently lost or gained a significant amount of weight?

   Yes   *No*

4. Has your appetite significantly increased or decreased for an extended period?

   Yes   *No*

5. Have your sleep habits changed significantly over the last two weeks (you may be having trouble sleeping or find you can't stay awake)?

   Yes   *No*

6. Have you noticed a significant drop in your energy level over the last two weeks?

   Yes   *No*

7. Do you consistently have feelings of worthlessness or disappointment for more than two weeks?

   Yes   *No*

8. Do you consistently have difficulty concentrating, thinking, or making decisions on a daily basis?

   Yes   *No*

9. Did you notice a negative change in your mood after a death or other specific event?

   Yes   *No*

10. Do you consistently have thoughts of death or suicide?

    Yes   *No*

* If you answered "Yes" to question 10, seek help as soon as possible.

HEALTHCARE PROVIDERS YOU NEED TO KNOW

There are a number of healthcare providers that are qualified to treat depression. Here is a list of them and what you can expect:

Christian Counselor (Ph.D.): These professionals have a doctoral degree. They have special training in using biblical principles and bringing The Holy Spirit into the counseling process/psychotherapy.

Psychologist: These professionals have a doctoral degree (Ph.D. or Psy.D.) in psychology. They area trained in psychotherapy, counseling, and psychological testing.

Psychiatrist (M.D.): These medical doctors specialize in the diagnosis and treatment of mental or psychiatric illnesses. They also offer psychotherapy and are licensed to prescribe drugs as part of their treatment.

Physician (M.D.): Your doctors (primary care physician, for example) have some training in treating and identifying mental or psychiatric problems. If you're symptoms are advanced, they can also refer you to another professional who specializes in your condition.

Physician Assistant: These medical practitioners have been trained to identify some psychiatric or mental disorders and can treat you under a physician's supervision. They can also make recommendations for other services that may help you.

Nurse Practitioner: These registered nurses (RNs) have additional training in nursing and can treat some mental or psychiatric disorders.

Licensed Counselor/Therapist, Social Worker (MA, MS): These professionals have a master's degree. These specialists provide mental health services for the prevention, diagnosis and treatment of depression and other mental or psychiatric conditions. They treat individuals, families, and groups to help them function and communicate more effectively.

Psychiatric Nurse Specialists (RNs): These registered nurses are educated in psychiatric nursing and they specialize in treating mental or psychiatric conditions.

CHAPTER THREE

Miracle Grow:
Relying on the Power of Prayer
to Cultivate Your Purpose in Life

MIRACLE GROW: ASSESSMENT STATEMENTS

Not at all				Very much
1	2	3	4	5

1. I read the Bible.

2. I pray daily.

3. I attend a Bible study or prayer group.

4. God is the center of my life.

5. I believe that God can give me power over my life.

mIRACLE GROW: PERSOnAL InUEnTORY

1. I can improve my relationship with the Lord by:

2. I can use the power of prayer when:

3. When I pray and read the Bible, I feel:

4. When I pray and worship with other men, I feel:

5. When I talk to God, I:

NOTE: You will find inventory questions throughout this book. Please take advantage of the space left open to you to jot down your own notes and personal thoughts as you move through the text. You may find it helpful to review your notes from time to time to assess your progress or revisit an idea at a later date.

JOURNEY TO THE DAY

Why does my comfort level decline and fall,
When I clasp my hands to pray?
Why does my heart race, my mind slip,
My eyes look away?
Surely, I'm not a non-believer,
I believe with all of my heart.
I trust in the winds and ways of our Father,
Yet, praise Him in the dark.

Journey to the day

When I am filled with Him
When I am resuscitated,
Rejuvenated by my alliance with Him.
When my soul at rest, knows.
When my taste for spiritual food is such,
The hunger won't let me go.

When I am altogether free of the tie that binds,
And am on my way.

To the day

To the day I find forgiveness, in the eyes of my Savior.

— **Larry Toussaint Garlington**

PRAYER POWER

In the first chapter, we looked at the importance of planting the right seed. And if you've inserted the right seed into fertilized soil, then you will have a great start—indeed! You're spiritually connected, have assessed how your family has impacted your future, expanded your education, enriched your social circle, and revamped your world view. But those aren't the only things you need to grow a healthy, productive future. Prayer is as necessary as the water you need to help a tree grow. It's not only a way for you to tell God what you need to fulfill your dreams; it's also a medium that God uses to communicate with you.

For many of us, prayer is something we rely on as a last resort. But if we look at the Bible, it encourages us to make prayer a part of our daily lives as a way to stay in constant conversation with the Father, whether it is in good times or bad. Here, you will be shown how to incorporate prayer into your life so that it impacts the very fabric of your existence. To do this, we'll first look at how you can realize your dreams through prayer and how those dreams can serve as an expression of your faith; discuss ways to strengthen your faith; look at examples of how people use prayer to change results; and point to specific scriptures in the Bible that emphasize the importance of prayer and faith.

VOICE OF EXPERIENCE #6

Steve grew up in the church. From the time he was eight years old, he remembered how the elders in the church would say, "Prayer changes things." Although he never questioned them, he never truly understood what they meant by that. He prayed, or at least that is what he thought he was doing. Yet, he was still having challenges at home and on the job. He turned to the Bible for answers but after the first few pages, he stopped reading it. A lot of the words were confusing to him and the story didn't really seem relevant. Besides that, he really didn't feel any emotional or spiritual connection to what he was reading and his frustration was leading him to stop going to church altogether. Then one day, he took a close look at the world around him and realized that prayer started with acknowledging God's presence and gifts. Steve was sitting alone in a park and he looked at the beauty of the trees and felt the warmth of the sun. He simply began talking to God openly and honestly, as if he were talking to a friend. When he returned to reading the Bible, he read without expectations and simply allowed the power of the words into his heart and mind. The Holy Spirit did the rest. Soon, Steve found himself making connections between his reading and solutions to problems in his life. He was able to trust God more and surrender without having to know all the answers.

We've all been in situations when we wonder if God truly hears us. Not only does God hear us during times of tribulation, He never stops listening. Keep believing that God hears us even when the circumstances fail to improve. God works on His timetable, not ours. So, we must take comfort in knowing that once we've turned our hopes, dreams, problems, or concerns over to the Lord, He is working them out for us. As the old folks say, He may not come when you want Him to but He is always on time. God will make the deadline, as long as you stop interfering, questioning, and worrying.

DREAM BIG

As a kid, football was my passion. One day, when I was 10, I went to an Army football game at West Point. I was in awe of West Point and totally amazed by the giant football players on the huge field. I remember looking at the stadium, inhaling and saying to myself, "I'm going to play here one day." I wasn't sure how

I was going to make it happen, but I just knew it would be a reality one day. God will make it happen.

In high school, I broke all the rushing records and was MVP in my league. The newspapers referred to me as, "the super back and the running back supreme." At Holy Cross College, the football team on which I was a player had a game on the exact same field. It hadn't occurred to me that I was actually living a dream that I had envisioned years earlier until our bus pulled up to West Point. I remember the feeling of a dream coming to fruition and it was an amazing sense of accomplishment, joy, and peace. But more than that, it was proof to me that my faith in God could make my wildest dreams come true. I could have chosen to attend any of the other colleges that had recruited me that didn't play at West Point, but because it was my destiny to play on that field on that particular day, God ordered my steps so that the impossible was made possible.

The whole time we played, I felt like I was walking on air. We won the game. I was MVP of the game, my team went on to win a national football championship and was ranked number one in the nation. But more importantly, I knew that I would be a winner in life because God had shown me that I could dream big and actually see those dreams come true.

Who cares if other people can't see what you see? There are some things that are for your eyes only. There are experiences, gifts, and circumstances that God has designed specifically for your development. Be glad that you have the possibility to see some things before other people do. That means you have faith (even if you didn't know it yet). Faith is the ability to see and believe in things when there is no real evidence, at least yet. Don't worry; the picture will come into view for everyone to see soon enough. For now, just sit back and enjoy the preview.

Just think of the most successful person that you know, whether it is personally or on television. That person's success started with a dream. It began with just a thought that was transformed into tangible results. The Bible contains a host of stories about things that happened as a result of a dream. Joseph responded to a dream warning that King Herod wanted to slay the Christ Child, so Joseph fled to Egypt where he hid the baby Jesus. And the Magi were warned in a dream not to tell King Herod of Jesus' whereabouts. There are other stories in the scriptures where people obediently follow God's orders as outlined in a dream. So, the connection between God and dreams is longstanding.

As for you, I encourage you to start envisioning your success. If you don't conceive it on the inside, you'll never be able to receive it on the outside. And when you build that image of your success, dream big. No matter how impossible that dream seems, you need to create it and make it real for you because if you don't have a dream, you'll never allow God to make a dream come true for you.

See yourself as being the premier husband, getting the best grades in your class, enjoying the fruits of a booming business, tripling your sales goals, landing the dream job, or doing whatever else you once thought was out of your reach. Think about your dreams constantly. Write down your thoughts. Tape yourself on a tape recorder. Draw pictures. Sketch out the images of your dreams. Speak of your dreams as if they've already come to pass and before you know it, your dreams will start to materialize. Believe it or not, the true measure of a man has nothing to do with how tall he is; it's the size of his dreams. And you can be a giant among men if you truly believe that.

And why wouldn't the impossible dream be possible for you? You have a relationship with Jesus Christ, and that means you've partnered with someone who's providing you with a blank check. God can cover anything that you can dream up, so be daring in your dreams, take risks, and be confident. Take comfort in knowing that God not only watches over us when we sleep, He's also able to help us realize the thoughts we've created when we are awake.

LOVE THE BLACK MALE WITHIN YOU

From an early age, I remember my mother always making me feel special. She constantly told us that we were special and I really came to believe it. I remember how that feeling affected me in school. When I went to first grade, I made a point of raising my hand in math class because my mother told us we had to let the teacher know when we could answer her questions. This was my mother's way of building our self-esteem and preparing us for racism. Initially, the teacher seemed surprised that I knew the information but after I proved myself, her expectations changed. Since my mother provided me with racial identity early on, I knew, despite what my teacher thought, I would prove my intellectual ability.

In addition to having a strong relationship with the Creator, there are three key components that you need to be aware of if you're ever going to fully love the Black male within you. They are: self-image, self-esteem, and racial identity. Your self-image is based on what you believe you look like physically, how you think your personality comes across to others, what kind of person you think you are, what you think others think of you, how much you like yourself, and how much you think others like you.

Since you were an infant, you have been constantly translating the various messages that you've received about yourself and your interpretation is reflected in your self-image. A positive self-image means that you've managed to put a positive spin on most of the information that you've received as a Black male.

Your self-image influences your self-esteem. That's the way you perceive your self-worth and how you feel about your self-image. If you feel positively about yourself, it's said that you have high self-esteem. Although nobody loves everything about themselves at all times, it's important that you feel positive about yourself most of the time because these feelings can have a direct impact on your success.

Racial identity is the personal significance you place on belonging to your particular racial group coupled with how you view that group on a social level. So if you received positive messages about Black people, then that helped shape your positive racial identity. In addition to affecting how you behave, racial identity impacts how others interact with you.

In 1971, researcher William Cross Jr. tried to further explain the significance of racial identity by using a five-stage model. It's helpful because it illustrates how the negative experiences of racism are transformed into a positive outlook. Briefly, it works like this: In stage one, the *pre-encounter stage*, a Black person believes in white superiority and rejects his Blackness. This person might participate in self-destructive behavior or do things that degrade his race. In stage two, the *encounter stage*, a Black person flips the script by adopting a pro-Black, anti-white philosophy.

Here, there is a passionate search for Black identity. Some outside event that destroyed his old perceptions usually triggers this new attitude. In the third stage, *immersion-emersion*, the person develops an overwhelming desire to understand the Black experience, African American history and the Black community. Though the individual may initially take on the "all whites are devils" stance, that mindset is altered as his Black rage fuses with reason. The focus then becomes community involvement and improvement. Stage four is *internalization* where the person does one of four things: 1) returns to their position in stage one; 2) becomes stuck in early stage three (immersed in white hatred); 3) becomes passive about racism and is content with showcasing a few pieces of Black paraphernalia; or 4) uses political involvement to implement change in the Black community. In stage five, *internalization commitment*, the person develops a sense of connectedness with all oppressed people. It's at this stage that Blacks develop a genuine concern for any human beings that are disadvantaged or mistreated. Self-esteem and racial identity are high. Most individuals go through the stages sequentially. Some people's development is arrested at a particular stage and they may stay there for an extended period of time.

Where are you in your development? If you haven't reached stage five yet, don't worry; you will progress. Unfortunately, the media is inundated with negative images of the Black male and many of us internalize those messages. But since you are a strong Black man in search of the truth, I know you'll be able to identify a lie when you see it.

Let's take the lie that describes Black men as endangered species, for example. According to the media, the *good Black man* is nearly nonexistent, but we know better. The term "endangered species" is usually related to animals. So in some sick way, the media is trying to reduce Black men to an "endangered animals"—the dodo bird, the humpback whale, and the dinosaur we see on television. They're trying to make us feel inferior and less than human beings. But what the media doesn't realize is that the term "endangered" could never apply to Black men. We've survived 400 years of slavery and we're moving forward as strong, healthy, extremely capable individuals. How can people who are "overcomers" by definition be endangered? They can't.

DEFINE YOURSELF AND CONTROL YOUR DESTINY

As long as we allow ourselves to let others control our own image, we will be portrayed in ways that demean us. As long as we rely on other people to tell our own truths, we will have to put up with the lies. That's just the way it works. When other people control the message, they also control the way the story is told and will usually tell it in a way that makes them look good. It is not in the media's best interest to portray us as the strong, powerful, progressive men that we are. People are much more interested in our shortcomings, foul-ups, mistakes, missteps, and misuses. And the consequences of what those messages are doing to the Black man's self-esteem are irrelevant. Things won't change in the media until we make them change. Considering our history, we shouldn't expect anything different.

So, what do we do about it? We do what we should have done a long time ago. We do what our mamas told us to do when they caught us in a lie. We tell the truth, our own truths. That way, when Black men are overwhelmed by the negative stereotypes that are used to describe them, they have the real story to rely on as a resource to help them be clear about who they are. We need to control our image and define ourselves. Most successful Black men in the media are rap artists, sports stars, and entertainers. I am proud of these brothers who have achieved their goals and financial success. However, successful Black men shouldn't be limited or regulated to these roles. Let's expand the view and exposure of who we are.

Just in case you need clarity, I'm going to take this opportunity to remind you of who you are:

YOU ARE THE FATHERS OF CIVILIZATION. We are the original people that God created on this earth and it's a fact that the African was the first human ever known. All scientific evidence points to the "African Eve" being the mother of all humans. Since this is the case, all people migrated from Africa to other lands. They left their homeland in response to food shortages, glacial melting, conflicts, and for other reasons. The migration resulted in groups of people settling in lands with various climates and environments. In many instances, the weather was much colder so the African features (such as dark skin, dark hair) were no longer necessary. Evidence of this process still exists today in some ancient countries.

Since we are the creators of all civilization, there is no need for us to ever feel like second-class citizens. Our ancestors paved the way for all people and all nations. God provided us with this responsibility because He loved us, valued us, and knew we were up for the challenge. We will not disappoint Him.

YOU ARE THE IMAGE OF CHRIST. Jesus Christ was a man of color. The word Christ comes from the Indian word "Krishna" or "Chrishna," which translates as "the Black One," as pointed out by Jeanette Davis-Adeshote in her book, *Black Survival in White America: From Past History to the Next Century.* And since Jesus was a man of color, it would stand to reason that his mother, the Virgin Mary, was also of color. Even the Pope has visited the Shrine of the Black Madonna in Poland.

At one time, Madonnas were always of color. But many Americans have converted the images of Jesus and the Virgin Mary to personify their white culture. White images of Jesus didn't emerge until 1505 when Pope Julius commissioned Michelangelo to paint biblical characters with European features. We send a very strong, conflicting message to Black people when we tell them to praise the white Jesus found in their churches when a very different physical description can be found in the Bible: "Jesus ... whose feet are like tarnished bronze ... " *(Rev. 2:18)*. Our churches should reflect the image of Jesus as He appears to us, as a Savior of our people in a way that best reflects who we are as a race.

YOU ARE ARTISTIC. Though the Romans and Greeks are considered great masters of architecture and art, many of their works replicate creations from Africa. Take the Pantheon in Athens, for instance. Although it is praised as one of the wonders of the world, *they* don't tell you it's a copy of Carnak Temple. This African religious site is three times the size of the Pantheon. In addition, the Roman and Grecian gods, goddesses, statues, fables, and myths were of African origin.

YOU ARE INVENTORS. Black people have created every type of gadget or process imaginable, including the watch (Benjamin Banneker), the heating system for New York's famous Radio City Music Hall and Rockefeller Center (David Crosthwait), the blood bank (Dr. Charles Richard Drew), meat curing products (Lloyd Augustus Hall), the Super Soaker (Lonnie Johnson), the gas mask (Garrett A. Morgan), the first medical textbook (Dr William Hinton), a chicken egg incubator (Granville T. Woods), and a street sweeper truck (Charles Brooks). It's impossible to think that we come from an inferior people when we come from a line of people that has created a long list of extraordinary developments. Now it's up to you to release the creative juices that are already housed in your spirit.

YOU ARE LEADERS. We're not just talking about the leaders that you know about such as Martin Luther King Jr., Marcus Garvey, Malcolm X, Elijah Muhammad or Farrakhan. But there is also Akhenaten, a Black Pharaoh in Egypt. His marriage to his wife, Nefertiti, changed the total belief system in Egypt from one that promoted "many gods" to the "one god" concept that is practiced by most Christians. As another example, Imhotep is the real father of medicine. He was a Black man from Ancient Egypt who lived about 2300 BC. Records show that the Greeks and Romans received much of their medical training from him. Despite what the history books may tell you, Hippocrates lived 2,000 years after Imhotep and is not the physician that provided the groundwork for today's medicine, as the Hippocratic oath implies.

And let's not forget the many Black men who go out to work every day to support their families. They are also leaders. Contrary to what the media tries to make you believe, most Black men are not in jail. As you know, the majority of us want to take care of our children, excel in the workplace, and live long lives so we can enjoy the fruits of our labor. We are active contributors to society on every level and we should reject any doctrine that fails to recognize that.

Of course, that's easier said than done. As stated in *Vision For Black Men* by Na'im Akbar, although Black men have played a very significant role in the evolution of human consciousness and religious and philosophical schools of thought, society makes it very difficult for us to access the information. "Our ancestors who laid the foundation left marks, symbols, indicators, [and] road maps," he writes. "They said, 'don't ever think that you can erase this. You can distort it, but you can't destroy it. [Europeans] have done all that they could do to pollute the air, and most of all, pollute your mind so that you look at yourself and don't know that it is you. They will go so far as to tell you that somebody from outer space created the great Egyptian monuments of civilization left in your homeland, Africa. That kind of thinking is madness of a world that does not want you to recognize your true identity.'" It's up to each of us to first find the truth and once we do that, we need to start sharing it with the community at large. The information I've provided here is only a small inkling of our greatness. Go to the library, visit your local bookstore, or search the Net to discover other interesting facts about our people. You'll learn so much about your Blackness, that you'll find it very difficult not to embrace it.

If you're still not ready to love yourself, then do it because you are a child of God. He made you perfect in His sight and if that's good enough for Him, that should be good enough for you too. You are unique. When you try to copy someone else or when you wish you were somebody else, you not only demean yourself, but you demean God's work. Regardless of what other people say or do, focus on being the person that God wants you to be. If you do that, you have no reason not to love the person that you are. It's only when you're "perpetrating a fraud," (do the young folks still say that?) being fake and not keeping it real that you become in danger of losing yourself and losing the special gifts that God made especially for you.

For true self-love, try seeing yourself in the same way that God sees you. His love is unconditional. He's not focusing on your shortcomings. He's not expecting you to dress, act, talk, or behave exactly like the brother next door. He doesn't care about the home runs you've missed, the many times you've been tackled along the way, the promotions that you never received, the number of women that turned you down on the dance floor, or any other things that may have brought you to your knees. God sees you as a winner because as long as you are His son, you couldn't be anything less.

If your child has difficulty on a test or loses a basketball game, what do you say? You probably say, "Learn from the experience and you'll do better next time." That's just how God is. Even when you fall short, His faith in you never wavers. "You'll get 'em next time," He cheers, because He knows the value that He's placed in you and you can never lose that value in His eyes. Besides, your faults provide God with an opportunity to do some of His best work. As long as you walk the earth, God is transforming, shaping, and molding you into the person that He wants you to be. When you make mistakes, you allow God to use those situations as lessons for you and others. You enable Him to prove that "you can do all things through Christ" *(Philippians 4:13)*. Beyond that, God also knows that loving someone requires that you love all of him or her, including the faults. Given all this, how could you not love yourself?

A host of benefits, opportunities and possibilities become available to you simply because you love yourself. You'll begin to talk about yourself in a loving manner. You'll get regular health examinations. You'll more closely monitor your behavior and abandon those things that disrespect you. You'll have high expectations of yourself and other people and you'll cut off the folks who fail to treat you properly. And no matter how many times someone else tells you that you're worthless, you'll know better because you'll be rooted in self-love and will have your own doctrine that defines who you are. Most importantly, you'll fully realize the dreams that God has planned for you because you'll believe that you deserve them.

LOVE THE LORD

If you want the benefits that come with having a relationship with God, then you must also **LOVE THE LORD**. The scriptures say, "thou shalt love the LORD thy God with all thine heart, and with all thy soul, and with all thy might" *(Deuteronomy 6:5)*. There doesn't seem to be much room for negotiation here. You must love the Lord to gain His favor. But God requires that you do more than just tell Him that you love Him; you must show Him through action.

One of the ways that you show you love the Lord is by making Him a priority. Just think about how you approached the dating game. There was that one girl whom you would call early in the week to make sure that you could take her out the following Saturday. She was the one you liked, the one you wanted to impress, the one you could see yourself having a long-term relationship with at some point. She wasn't the lady in waiting that you'd only call at the last minute or whenever the girl you really wanted to go out with was busy. You treated them differently because your interest in each of them was different. The same is true for how you treat God. If you truly love Him, you wouldn't turn to Him at the last minute after all of your attempts to solve a problem have failed, would you? You'd share your resources with God, if you loved Him. They say you can see where a man's heart is by looking at where he spends his time and money. Look at how much time you spend enjoying the presence of the Lord. If you spend more time watching ESPN's *Sports Center* than you do connecting with God and family, that's probably not a good sign. Also, if you love the Lord, then you'll spend your money in places that will edify Him. According to the Bible, "For where your **treasure is**, there will your heart be also" *(Matthew 6:21)*.

Count your blessings and thank God continually. Humans just want to be appreciated and God does too. When we express our gratitude to Him, it makes Him smile. Rick Warren's *The Purpose Driven Life* (Zondervan, 2002) says our willingness to praise God for His goodness also benefits us. "An amazing thing happens when we offer praise to and thanksgiving to God," writes Warren. "Worship works both ways. We enjoy what God has done for us, and when we express that enjoyment to God, it brings Him joy but it also increases our joy."

Use the gifts God has provided us as another way to express our love for Him. So if we have special abilities to sing, write, paint, lead, speak, build, create, mend, or support, for example, we should use these skills or we run the risk of losing them. More importantly, we prevent God from enjoying the special gifts that He has given us. As long as we're not using God's gifts for sin, the Lord is as delighted as we are when we allow ourselves to enjoy our divine gifts (and we're not just talking for use in the church here). Use your talents where you can, whenever you can, as a testament to God's good works.

In your quest to love God, obey God. This is a tough one. As much as we say that the Bible is a book of truth, how many of us follow it as if it is the truth. A lot of times, we pick and choose the principles that we're going to follow. But partial obedience is not the same as full obedience. Follow His word and as you grow in faith, it becomes easier. Having a personal relationship with God and loving Him with all of your heart and soul is most important.

Everything God does and says applies to us and we need to believe that He is always operating in our best interest. Our love of God should convince us to trust Him completely. If you do that, then you know that your dreams will come true because He said He would deliver in His word. *Matthew 7:7* says, "Ask, and it shall be given you; seek, and ye shall find; knock, and it shall be opened unto you." Whatever request you've made of God has already been fulfilled; now it's up to you to truly believe that.

BELIEVE IN THE POWER OF THE LORD

Just as you've planted your seeds for growth, God plants seeds in you. He's constantly trying to convince you to give up your old ways, let go of past inhibitions, and be open to new and exciting opportunities. But unless you have faith, God's seeds will never take root. You'll never truly understand the depth of God's love or the extent of his influence. He really has the whole world in His hand.

But how do you start believing in something that you've never believed? This "faith thing" may be completely new to you. If you're used to handling things yourself, it's difficult to place something in the Lord's hands when you haven't done that in the past. You bet it is. But there are things in life that only make sense in reverse. So, once you pray, God delivers, and everything is all good, you'll say, "Oh, that's what Ernest meant." The thing to do at this point is put things in God's hands even if you don't fully believe in the outcome. According to the Bible, your faith only needs to be the size of a mustard seed to get results. Surely, you can drum up at least that much faith.

There are other things you can do to increase your faith. Of course, none of them will be effective if you're not open to them. But if you are willing to consider suggestions, try these:

READ HIS WORD. One of the first things you can do to increase your faith is to start reading the Bible on a daily basis. Ideally, take time out to read it in the morning and at night. It's a wonderful reference book because it provides guidance in every aspect of our lives. Anything that you are experiencing has happened in the Bible and if you read it, you'll be given advice on how you should handle the situation today. The Bible tells us that if we seek God, we will find Him *(Matthew 7:7)*. It also promises us that God will transform us as long as we allow it *(Romans 12:2)*. As He transforms us, He'll transform our disbelief as well and allow us to trust Him. Indulge in God's word, for understanding and insight.

RECOGNIZE TRUTH. Jesus Christ shows you who He is on a moment-by-moment basis, so believe Him. There really is no fancy way to convert your disbelief to belief. The shortest way to believe is simply to believe. The Bible commands us to "believe in the Lord Jesus Christ, and thou shalt be saved." There's no room for negotiation here.

LOOK FOR PROOF. As we go about our lives, there are solutions and opportunities that can only be explained because we know that God intervened on our behalf. Whether we actually prayed for it, we need to give God credit and acknowledge Him for the things He's already doing in our lives. According to *1 Peter 1:7*, these situations are specifically designed for our acknowledgment. It says He uses challenges to make us stronger Christians.

KEEP COMPANY WITH PEOPLE WHO HAVE FAITH. Birds of a feather really do flock together. If you surround yourself with people who have a high degree of faith, their positive energy will rub off on you.

Talk to people who have strong faith. Don't just hang out with people who have faith. Talk to them about their faith and be ready to listen to these stories repeatedly. Many times we are moved to believe things just because we hear the same things so often. The more you hear stories or scriptures on faith, the more likely you are to start increasing your faith. According to the Bible, "faith comes from listening to the message of Good News about Christ" *(Romans 10:17)*.

LISTEN TO THE TESTIMONY FROM OTHERS. Sometimes you can increase your faith by relying on an interpretation from someone else. For example, I have never been to England, but I believe that the country exists because I believe the testimony provided by others. I have never died but I believe that I will die because of the many people who have died before me. By the same token, you can increase your faith in God by focusing on what God has done for other people. Listen to people who tell you how God saved them, pardoned their sins, changed their character, and helped them rebuild their lives. As you hear numerous stories of faith and proof, you'll be moved to believe that those possibilities will exist for you as well.

LET GO, LET GOD

At one time, I wasn't one to talk about faith and the power of prayer. In my early twenties, worrying nearly consumed me. I took a close look at why I worried so much. A lot of it was due to some bad childhood habits that I picked up. My mom worried a great deal when I was growing up. She wanted desperately to financially care for her children but felt overwhelmed. The money didn't stretch far enough and we frequently went without heat or clothing. Often, we were evicted from our apartments. Of course, these things provided my mom with a great deal of anxiety and I began to share her stress, almost out of a sense of duty. In fact, I thought you were supposed to worry. I even thought it meant that you were somehow a more compassionate person if you worried. But that habit became detrimental to my health. It led to ulcers, headaches, and the same feelings of anxiety that my mother experienced. I later found out that worrying is a sin because if you truly believe that God is in charge, then there is no need to worry. I asked the Lord to take this bad habit from me and I felt the Holy Spirit telling me that if I prayed and was going to continue to worry, then I shouldn't pray. God removed that demon from my spirit and I'm happy to say He changed my worrying spirit to one of great faith. He can do the same for you as long as you believe that He can make a difference and be true to His word.

TURN TO THE SCRIPTURES

Still need some inspiration to help you understand the power of prayer and increase your faith? No problem. It's all in the good book. Feed your spirit by referring to these selections of scriptures for daily encouragement or comfort in your time of need.

Now faith is the substance of things hoped for, the evidence of things not seen. For by it the elders obtained a good report. Through faith we understand that the worlds were framed by the word of God, so that things which are seen were not made of things which do appear *(Hebrews 11:1-3)*.

For we walk by faith, not by sight *(2 Corinthians 5:.7)*.

Whatsoever is not of faith is sin *(Romans 14:23b)*.

God hath dealt to every man the measure of faith *(Romans 12:3b)*.

So then faith cometh by hearing, and hearing by the word of God *(Romans 10:17)*.

By faith Abel offered unto God a more excellent sacrifice than Cain, by which he obtained witness that he was righteous, God testifying of His gifts: and by it he being dead yet speaketh *(Hebrews 11:4)*.

...for verily I say unto you, If ye have faith as a grain of mustard seed, ye shall say unto this mountain, Remove hence to yonder place; and it shall remove; and nothing shall be impossible unto you *(Matthew 17:20)*.

But the fruit of the Spirit is love, joy, peace, longsuffering, gentleness, goodness, faith *(Galatians 5:22)*.

We are bound to thank God always for you, brethren, and rightly so, because that your faith growth exceedingly, and the charity of every one of you all toward each other aboundeth; So that we ourselves glory in you in the churches of God for your patience and faith in all your persecutions and tribulations that ye endure *(II Thessalonians 1:3-4)*.

Faith will carry us through every trial and tribulation. Faith is really not that difficult. God made it easy. In essence, faith is just taking one more step with Jesus; it's believing God for one more hour, and because we do not give up on God, He comes through with our answers when we trust Him.

BROTHER"HOOD" AND GROUP PRAYER

Recognize that prayer will help us overcome and gain strength and power in any situation. The oral tradition that is so strong for us as Black men needs to be perpetuated and embraced. Talk and pray with one another. Empower one another and hold each other accountable through prayer. Ask God for strength and guidance and pray together to give each other strength and guidance, then follow through with making sure that you are able to honor your commitments. Set goals and check in with each other to make sure that you are taking small, concrete steps to reach the short-term goals to ultimately get to your long-term goal. Support churches and recognize that there is a destiny between God and us. There is a divine plan for our highest good. Create a covenant between us, a group of praying men and God. There's healing that happens through prayer and it's particularly through group prayer. Jesus talked about this when He said, "When two or more are gathered in my name I am going to be present." There's a multiplication of prayer and power. If you want it and you need it, pray for it, work for it, and God will provide it. He will provide what is best for us in His time. The more we decrease ourselves, the more the Christ and the Lord increase in our lives. God guides us to be able to love ourselves as Christians and the Christ within us more than we love ourselves as men of this world. We will be able to focus on and gain power and strength from Christ's spirit within us. The more that we try to be like Christ, the more we love who we truly are. This only comes from the power of prayer. The Lord says, "My burden is light." When we focus on the Lord taking over our burdens, He is the redeemer.

Intercessory prayer with one another is fundamental. This involves being able to get together and pray that God will intercede and that we can support each other in our goals and our objectives. A group approach offers not just spiritual brother"hood" but accountability. **The ultimate goal of this chapter is to encourage Black men to initiate group Bible studies**. It could be two people; it doesn't matter how small the group is.

I knew from the first moment I met Bob Jacks that I would absorb wisdom from him. He said, "Ernest, I would like to invite you to a Bible study with a group of Christian men who are prayer warriors." I immediately responded, "Absolutely, I would love to come." At my first meeting with the Bible study group I knew in an instant that it was my destiny to gain knowledge from the process because this was a unique Bible study. It was actually a Bible support group that focused on encouraging men to reach their goals and take action in their lives; to overcome the challenges; to accomplish goals and fulfill their purpose in life. My new knowledge would allow me to encourage Black men to establish Bible studies through which empowerment of one another through Christ would be possible.

We will deepen our spiritual connection with each other during this process. Encourage this movement to spread throughout our nation. We will empower each other and gain power over our destiny. Envision these Bible studies from basements to vast Web sites. Be as creative as possible. Connect in the workplace, sporting arenas, street corners, and even in a club. Find a place to pray wherever you are. It doesn't matter what type of lifestyle you are currently living—whether you are a CEO, drug dealer or user, student, unemployed, a prisoner, a professional athlete, an entertainer, an entrepreneur—because the Lord will lead you where you need to be, and change you in ways that you need to be changed. This is an aggressive approach and relationship with God. There is a holy war within the spirit of our people. We will talk about the Lord and His Word wherever we are. The Lord will permeate through anything and everywhere. We will lovingly challenge each other to take action toward our goals. As we do this, our spirits will grow strong. The key to our movement is the connection between brothers. Our strength comes from being spiritually with God.

Every Black man should have a Bible. If you have not read one page of the Bible or if you have read it in its entirety, take the time to buy a Bible for yourself and another brother. Give the Bible to your brother and tell him you love him. Read it and share the word. Carry your Bible with you at all times. May God continue to guide you in gaining power over your life.

CHAPTER FOUR

Eliminating the Weeds & Poison Vines: Combating Oppression, Racism and Self-Destructive Behavior

---

ELIMINATING THE WEEDS & POISON VINES: ASSESSMENT STATEMENTS

Not at all   **Very much**
  1   **2**   **3**   **4**   **5**

1. I work at not allowing racism to stop me from achieving my goals.

2. I try to avoid self-destructive behavior.

3. I can name significant accomplishments made by African American men in history.

4. I am knowledgeable about slavery and its impact on our people.

5. I recognize the pain that we as African American men experience and I am passionate about the healing process.

ELIMINATING THE WEEDS & POISON VINES: PERSONAL INVENTORY

1. The best way to heal myself is:

2. I can help heal other Black men by:

3. Five ways I gain power over racism are:

4. I rely on my relationship with God to help me heal by:

5. I dispel stereotypes about Black men by:

NOTE: You will find inventory questions throughout this book. Please take advantage of the space left open to you to jot down your own notes and personal thoughts as you move through the text. You may find it helpful to review your notes from time to time to assess your progress or revisit an idea at a later date.

S
T
A
N
D

A grieving Mother Africa speaks to her children.
To her sons and daughters torn from her breast.
Coerced into conforming to lifetimes of degradation.
Forced to forget their lineage.
Their heritage,
Their culture,
The wondrous history that makes the black one proud.
Her children were contaminated with untruths.
Blinded by systematic schools of darkness.
Still recovering from conditions so cold and tragedies so
terrific,
That world wars pale in comparison.
Mother Africa feels in her heart that the time is right.
Her children have grown, are seasoned and bright.
Ready-made warriors seeking the truth that only dignity, pride
and self awareness can deliver.
Mother Africa speaks to,
Beckons the African American,
To Stand

Stand! If you have ever dueled against the mighty ministers of
racism.
Stand! If you have absorbed their blows and forged forward
with fortitude and grace.

If you feel for our fathers and mothers who slaved in the fields,
with sweat on their brow and blood on their back.

Then stand, for your family,
And prepare your offspring to reap the riches of the sun.
Be wonderful and unwavering.
Like a sculpture made of rock.
Like a steel boned skyscraper built to endure.
Like a prized champion, poised and confident.
Never lay down.

S
T
A
N
D

Black Man

— **Larry Toussaint Garlington**

Wherefore if thy hand or thy foot offend thee, cut them off, and cast them from thee: it is better for thee to enter into life halt or maimed, rather than having two hands or two feet to be cast into everlasting fire *(Matthew 18:8)*.

And if thine eye offend thee, pluck it out, and cast it from thee: it is better for thee to enter into life with one eye, rather than having two eyes to be cast into hell fire *(Matthew 18: 9)*.

God is very direct when it comes to dealing with things that halt our progress. According to Him, if there is anything that is preventing us from successfully reaching His kingdom, we need to cut it off. Just think, He's telling us that it's better to walk the earth half blind than to keep an eye that offends *Him*. That's just how serious He wants us to be when we assess ourselves as individuals, as a race and as a nation.

If we find ourselves in the company of racists. Head them off at the pass, cut them off at the knees, and stomp out their negativity. The Bible tells us that in Christ, we are more than conquerors. As we wage this war against racism, we prepare ourselves for battle.

We are spiritual warriors. Our wounds make us stronger. We'll turn those wounds into weapons of mass determination. When we see blood, we'll fight harder spiritually. Though we are fully prepared to die for what we believe in, we also know Black men are invaluable and we understand that life is a precious gift from God. The only battles we should involve ourselves in are those that are essential for the betterment of our community and the glory of the Father.

Our past makes it easy for us to give our lives. Racism attempted to devalue us to the point where our lives had so little value that death was meaningless. Our inner pain and the things we've dealt with as African Americans caused us to look at death as a sign of relief rather than the ultimate sacrifice. But now, we battle for a clear purpose and we will forge ahead until our mission is accomplished.

In this chapter, we'll determine how we can conquer all of the things that interfere with our development as a people and as individuals. This requires that we devise a plan to address institutional racism, historical atrocities, and the terrorist acts that have been conducted against our people. As Americans, we have a Constitutional right to defend our families against these horrific crimes of oppression. On an individual level, we'll take an honest look at the self-defeating nature of Black-on-Black/intraracial hatred and envy that exists in our own community. All of these areas are important because until we can begin to weed out the negativity that surrounds us, we will never be able to realize our full potential.

UOICE OF EHPERIENCE #7

Ted was a manager of a department store and he always had an excuse for being irresponsible. "The white man is holding me down," he would say. Consequently, he was passed up for a promotion. Ted blamed his supervisor and requested a meeting with the human resources director, who happened to be African American also. As Ted told him about his frustration and resentment at being passed over, the supervisor reviewed documents on his desk. When Ted had completed his tirade, the director stated the number of times Ted had been late to work, the number of times he called in sick, and the complaints filed against him by both the Black and white people that he supervised. He told him in a supportive but firm tone that he could not blame his white supervisor for holding him down if he did not show reliable and responsible behavior. If Ted's supervisor was racist, Ted had given him every opportunity to hold him back. Although Ted was initially angry and defensive, he had to do some introspection and look at his behavior. He was able to gain insight into his behavior and recognize that he acted out in self defeating ways when he felt someone was mistreating him. In fact, even as a young man, Ted would sabotage his grades and academic achievement when he was angry with the teacher. Acknowledging this pattern was the first step toward change.

EXPLORING THE PAST AS A PATHWAY TO THE FUTURE

As stated earlier, Africans are the parents of all civilization. The world evolved into a melting pot as a result of various groups of people migrating to different areas for survival or exploration. The features of each of those groups changed in response to their environment. Race was not used as a means to discriminate as it is today. Race only became a factor when it was economically profitable to enslave people for free labor. The Europeans enslaved the Africans because they spoke a different language and would be easily identifiable. The Africans were only called *inferior* and *less human* to clear the conscience of the slave owners who needed to explain how they could subject other human beings to such cruel and abusive treatment. Contrary to the history books, the Africans were intelligent, hardworking individuals who were very content with their homeland. Africa was rich in resources, so its inhabitants were well fed.

During the slave trade, Africans were first shipped to the Caribbean, where they were then sent to their final destinations. Some of the places accepting slaves were Brazil, Europe, French Caribbean, British Caribbean, Dutch Caribbean, Central and South America, Mexico, Canada, and the United States. Overall, more than nine million slaves were stolen from Africa. All slaves went through the Caribbean so there really is no basis for dissension between Blacks in the United States versus Blacks in the Caribbean. All of us are originally from the African continent, so we are all brothers and sisters.

The slaves in America were particularly mistreated. They were subjected to being beaten, underfed, and chained. Despite three centuries of servitude, the slaves still attempted to hold onto their

---

In a recent column by Archie Richards, "Government policies don't help blacks," he asserts that big-government policies have hurt blacks more than they have helped. He sites the following policies to support his statement:

- The Davis-Bacon Act was enacted in the 1930s specifically to give whites preference over Blacks in obtaining high-paid, unionized construction jobs. Outrageously, the law remains in effect.

- Minimum Wage Laws make it especially difficult for Black men in central cities to obtain jobs. Economist Milton Friedman calls minimum wages "the most racist laws on the books."

- Welfare: Until the mid-1990s, welfare laws provided living wages for mothers. But the mothers were required not to work and not to marry an employed man. Therefore, millions of children have grown up without fathers in an environment of dependency.

- Many of the above laws were passed with good intentions. As is usually the case with big-government policies, the actual, long-term results are opposite. Most Americans are not racist, but some of the nation's laws are.

music, customs, and affinity for the African continent. Because of their conscious decision and determination to maintain at least some connection to their heritage, we still have many of our ancestral ties.

You see it in our dance, drumming, singing, and rhythmic movements. Africa is present in our women when they don African garb or braided hairstyles. The Motherland is present in our religious experience as we praise God through song, handclapping, and foot stomping as we do what God has commanded of us: Make a joyful noise unto the LORD, all the earth: make a loud noise, and rejoice, and sing praise *(Psalms 98:4)*.

There's no denying that slavery left a negative impact on Black men, leaving residual effects of a slave mentality, causing some of us to use the white man as a "crutch" or an excuse that prevents us from taking full power and responsibility over our lives. There has also been a loss of education and language. And slavery largely contributed to the destruction of the Black family, abuse, and other destructive behaviors, and the generational demons that still plague us. But slavery is also a reminder that even in the worst of circumstances, we refuse to let other people steal our joy.

VOICE OF EXPERIENCE #8

Byron struggled when he decided to stop selling drugs and get a job. His struggles were related to his criminal lifestyle and doing whatever he needed to survive. After going to jail and living through the gangsta *lifestyle, he concluded that this way of life wasn't working for him, and he desired legitimate employment.*

Although he did manage to get a job, Byron's greatest challenge was losing a group of friends who said, "You think you're better than us? You can't hang on the block anymore?" Sometimes, when his supervisor at work put him down, he would start thinking negatively. "I don't need this hassle," he'd think. "I don't have to do this. I can go out and sell drugs and make a lot more money and get more respect." The internal struggles forced him to shift his understanding of strength as a Black male. He became proud of getting up at 4:00 a.m. and getting to work by 6:00. He began to recognize the strength it takes to deal with a stressful work environment and then go home and get ridiculed by his friends who continued to say, "Hey, you're not making any money. If you're working, where's your money at?" Losing friends and living through this transition took a total reconfiguration of his identity. Byron would tell himself, "I'm strong and I'm going to work and I'm going to do the right thing and I'm going to get myself out of this life. I don't like the idea of being chased by the police, hurting the community, and living off of sickness in addiction. It's simply not how I want to live my life anymore."

Byron decided to start taking classes because he didn't like factory work. He began taking classes at a community college, studying to become a CPA. He was motivated to do it and paid for his own classes. He is now coaching a kids' basketball team, which is something that he always wanted to do but couldn't because he was selling drugs. The main thing, Byron says, is that he feels better about himself now than he ever has. To gain power over his life, he improved the way he felt about himself and truly began to develop a strong sense of African American male identity in a positive way. Byron still remembers feeling that he couldn't survive without drugs during his first year of working as he struggled with his bills, and how easy it would be to go back to selling drugs because that was what he knew and it had been his only source of income for so long. He also remembers feeling trapped, that there was no way out of that lifestyle. But through his personal strength and working hard for three years, he had improved his credit and purchased a beautiful townhouse.

STAYING FOCUSED AND MOBILIZED

Instead of looking at slavery as a source of embarrassment, use the pain of our past as a power source. Think about the struggles of our forefathers and look at their successes. You come from a legacy of thinkers, planners, and achievers. Have a great sense of pride when you think of all that our brothers and sisters have accomplished in the face of such intense tribulation. At the same time, know that you bear a great sense of responsibility because you need to continue the charge set forth by our ancestors. It's your turn to make your mark in the history books. What will you do with the time that you have remaining?

Pray for the answer. Take some time out to meditate on what God's will is for your life. Being still can be a good thing as long as you use the time wisely. Try fasting and praying as a way to expedite the process of being able to get centered and focused on hearing God's guidance and being able to follow His divine wisdom and plan for you. Worship Him. Use every part of you to focus on Him. In doing that, you will gain a greater understanding of yourself from a mental, emotional, and spiritual perspective. You'll also come to know how you can become more like the Christ you worship and love.

CONFRONTING THE THINGS THAT HURT US

Since Africans came to the Americas as slaves, there have been groups of people that have consciously devised schemes to destroy us. It's up to us to identify these poisons, weed them out and make it nearly impossible for them to take root in the future. This is the short list, but you get the idea and can spread the word about other destructive forces you know about:

• **THE KKK:** Originally, the Ku Klux Klan (KKK) referred to itself as a Protestant white-supremacist fraternal organization and was created in 1865 in opposition of slave reform policies in the South. The group often used terrorism and violence to express its disapproval and although the original organization was supposedly disbanded by 1880, the KKK has re-emerged in various forms. Later sects of the KKK forged attacks against Roman Catholics, Asians, Jews, Blacks, and other immigrants in the United States. At its peak in the 1920s, the KKK had four million members before it was again disbanded during War World II in 1944. Another KKK group cropped up in the 1960s to oppose the Civil Rights Act and you can still get KKK T-shirts and other paraphernalia today.

• **POLICE BRUTALITY:** In 1991, Rodney King became a symbol of police brutality against Black men when an amateur videotape was widely televised. It showed police officers brutalizing King after a car chase. In April 1992, the four white LAPD police officers were acquitted of assault and an uprising broke out in response. In Los Angeles, scores of fires were set and stores were looted. The riots spread throughout the United States in smaller cities. Most recently, a young man in New York City was shot by a police officer on the roof of his apartment building. The officer was not convicted for the incident. Police violence against Black men remains alive.

• **THE PRISONS:** To date, there are more African American males in prison than there are in advanced educational institutions and the military. The American prison system is a billion-dollar business and has many characteristics that liken it to modern-day slavery. Since 1980, there has been a staggering increase in the Black male prison population. As a result, a large sector of our community is absent from caring for their families, participating in the American political system, and achieving their dreams. We must demand correctional facilities that truly rehabilitate, that allow prisoners a chance to educate themselves and prepare for employment rather than banish them from the job market.

KNOWING YOUR RIGHTS

A primary goal of the Civil Rights Movement was to change laws so that Black people could more fully participate in the democratic process and be treated fairly. After the Civil War, specific laws had to be instituted to abolish slavery. Then, the Constitution had to be amended to give Blacks the right to vote and provide them with the same rights as their white counterparts. But that was only the beginning; once the Constitution was changed, civil rights leaders worked hard to ensure that America delivered what the Constitution promised. Familiarize yourself with the law so that you know your rights as an American citizen and as a Black person. As a reminder, I'm including some monumental occurrences that largely impacted our history:

• **MISSOURI COMPROMISE** (1820) enabled each state to determine whether it would permit slavery. It was designed to maintain an even number of slave and free states. It helped keep the peace between the two until the Civil War.

• **KANSAS-NEBRASKA ACT** (1854) abolished the Missouri Compromise. The fighting associated with this act became known as "Bloody Kansas."

• **DRED SCOTT DECISION** (1857) was one of the many arguments that resulted in the Civil War. Dred Scott was born a slave in 1795 and was later sent to John Emerson's plantation. When Emerson, a surgeon in the U.S. Army, was reassigned to the free state of Illinois, he took Scott with him. When the two ultimately returned to Missouri (a slave state), Emerson died. Scott then requested his freedom from his owner's widow and was denied. In 1846, Scott sued the family for his freedom, claiming that the years he spent in free territory made him a free United States citizen. After a ten-year battle, the Supreme Court ruled that Blacks had no rights to sue because they were considered property and not covered under the United States Constitution. The following year, Scott died a slave. The Supreme Court decision angered the people in the free states, which helped fuel the Civil War.

• **THE PRESIDENCY OF ABRAHAM LINCOLN** (1860-1865). The sixteenth president faced one of the greatest challenges in United States history. After his election, the Southern states (which were mostly Democrat at the time) were afraid things would significantly change so they attempted to secede from the Union and start a new country. To save the Union, Lincoln started the Civil War in 1861. Then, in 1863, Lincoln set forth a punishment to the seceding states by putting the Emancipation Proclamation into effect. It freed the slaves in all areas controlled by the Confederacy. The North won the war, slavery was abolished in all states, and Lincoln gave his famous Gettysburg Address in 1863. On April 4, 1865, Lincoln became the first assassinated president in the United States. He was 56 years old.

• **CIVIL WAR AMENDMENTS:** *The Thirteenth* (1865),

Fourteenth (1868), and *Fifteenth* (1870) amendments were important changes to the U.S. Constitution because they gave Black activists the right to push for change during the Civil Rights Movement. The Thirteenth Amendment ended slavery in the United States. The Fourteenth Amendment gave Blacks the same rights as whites. The Fifteenth Amendment gave Blacks the right to vote in the United States.

• **RECONSTRUCTION** (1865-1877) was the period following the Civil War when laws were made to provide Blacks with more rights. This period lasted for about twelve years.

• **PLESSY *v* FERGUSON** (1892) made it legal to segregate cars, trains, and buses. Homer Plessy, a 30-year-old arrested for sitting in a car for whites only on the East Louisiana Railroad, believed that the "separate but equal" law violated the Thirteenth and Fourteenth amendments. He argued that separatism made it impossible for Blacks to be treated equal to whites. The white cars were nicer and cleaner than the Black cars. Ultimately, the Supreme Court ruled that Plessy wasn't being treated unequally, just separately. Even though Plessy lost his case and was put in jail, the impact of the Plessy v Ferguson case was monumental. The ruling lead to separate restrooms, restaurants, theaters, and public schools. It took 64 years before the "separate but equal" law was ruled unconstitutional under the Brown v Board of Education decision.

• **BROWN *v* BOARD OF EDUCATION** (1954) The Supreme Court ruled that separate was not equal in the public school system in Topeka, Kansas. Under this ruling, segregation in schools became illegal.

- **THE CIVIL RIGHTS ACT OF 1964:** President John F. Kennedy made great strides to end segregation. During his term in office, he appointed Black people to roughly 40 federal positions. He also chose five Black federal judges, providing new encouragement for the Black community at large. The 1964 Civil Rights Act made it illegal to force Blacks to use separate facilities at theaters, schools, restrooms, restaurants, buses, and trains.

KEEPING OUR EYES ON THE PRIZE

So what does this all mean? Just like the many people before us, this generation must demand what is best for our community and be committed to improving this country and its conditions. There's a great lie being circulated that tries to separate the Black man from America. But you need to understand that we are absolutely part of her history and culture. We have built this nation through our ancestors' slave labor and turned this land into the mighty financial, military and political power that it is.

We must declare that we're going to transform our nation, our countrymen, and ourselves so that we can elevate the Christian Spirit of America. I implore you to pray daily about this. Believe it in your heart, spirit, mind, and soul. This is our mission that has been given to us by the Almighty and it's up to each one of us to make it a reality for us and generations to come.

In the meantime, be very clear about the issues that face us today:

AFFIRMATIVE ACTION is responsible for bringing Blacks closer to being in parity with their white counterparts. But we still have more progress to make in this area because white America has gotten a 400-year head start. As

Jeanette Davis-Adeshote points out in her book, *Black Survival in White America: From Past History to the Next Century* (Bryant & Dillon, 1995), the system isn't doing nearly enough. "The fact that Blacks have been patient for so long is amazing," she writes. "They have compromised with legislators to make it as fair for whites as possible, yet, whites being used to having 'it all,' do not want to comply. Just as everyone has to sacrifice for deficit reduction, it would have been commendable if whites had agreed to do the same to bring Blacks in parity with them in the 1960s. Maybe by now Affirmative Action would be less needed." We still need it and it should be rigorously implemented.

REPARATION is a term used to indicate that Blacks should be compensated for their 400 years of free labor. As our brother Spike Lee points out, we never even received the forty acres and a mule that were promised to us after the emancipation of the slaves. Reparation is not about getting a handout, as whites (and even some Blacks) imply; it's about repaying a debt. America owes Black people and they need to compensate Blacks for the mental, physical, and financial devastation that were imposed on them. Beyond that, reparation, the act of making a group of people whole as a result of a grave injustice, is not a new concept. Reparation was paid to the Native Americans for the acts perpetrated by the pilgrims; the Japanese for the time they spent in camps during World War II; and the Jews were also compensated for their losses during the Holocaust. America owes us too and it's time she pay up.

EDUCATION is key to our community's progress. As we discussed earlier, making changes to the Constitution is key to improving our existence in the United States. Most recently, Congressman Jesse Jackson Jr. is directing his efforts to amend the Constitution so that quality education becomes a right for all Americans. If successful, Jackson would ensure that education be taken from state jurisdiction and be put under federal rule, forcing the nation to make the educational system a unified, standard system. Should this occur, all public schools would have access to the same federal funds. For minorities and low-income Americans, this would be ideal because it would provide them with equal access to higher quality schools or at least give them a legal basis for compelling the United States to raise the standard for schools in underserved neighborhoods. Although a national educational restructure isn't something that could happen overnight, the congressman says amending the Constitution is a necessary first step. For now, African Americans should continue the fight for quality education on a local level and stay abreast of Jackson's progress (www.jessejacksonjr.com).

WATCHING THE COMPANY YOU KEEP

A brother in California recalls the first day he realized how important it was to be selective of his friends and associates. "I was probably no more than nine years old," he explains, "and I was hanging out with the guys on the block as they were acting a fool. It was fine until one of the *fellas* decided to run down to the corner house and climb up Mrs. Drake's tree to snatch one of her red apples. It didn't seem like a very big deal at the time. After all, Mrs. Drake had a tree full of apples. But that didn't stop her from running straight to my mother's house to tell her that I was involved in some unauthorized apple picking. I explained to her and my mom that even though I saw who did it and knew the guy who did it, I wasn't the one who stole the apple and I didn't have anything to do with the incident. At that time my mother explained to me that I was *guilty by association* and I got grounded for a week for merely being around when the mischief was being done. Well, needless to say, I stopped hanging around those cats. And it was a good thing, because the next new friend they made was accidentally shot and killed because he was mistaken for one of the other males in the group."

UOICE OF EHPERIENCE #9

Lonnie's uncle, an alcoholic, had sexually abused him as a child. Lonnie had kept the abuse a secret into adulthood. Although he was heterosexual, he harbored feelings of shame that he had felt physically stimulated when his uncle touched him. Lonnie spent years avoiding genuine friendships with men and emotionally intimate relationships with women, even though he eventually married. He feared that his secret would eventually be revealed in his interactions. In order to heal, Lonnie had to face the demons of his past and begin the process of not blaming himself and forgiving his uncle. After a devastating divorce, Lonnie forced himself to take steps toward healing. He told his mother what had happened to prepare her for the aftermath of confronting his uncle. The confrontation ended up being very different from what Lonnie had imagined. When his uncle opened the door, Lonnie saw a man who had aged, the ravages of alcohol taking its toll. Although Lonnie was able to express his anger and pain, the intensity was not what he had imagined it would be. His uncle did not say much, neither admitting nor denying the abuse. All he said was, "I never wanted to hurt you." Lonnie thought it was weak, but only felt pity for his uncle. However, after 30 years of pain, the healing had begun.

Slave holders controlled, abused, and mistreated Black men. After slavery, Black men were tortured, beaten, and lynched. Racists murdered Black men. There was justifiable rage, public outcry and political movements to combat these injustices. Now, Black men are being shot daily.

We are being killed in numbers parallel to those despicable periods in history. The difference is we are killing each other. The *gangsta* mentality that permeates our community is self-destructive and indicative of self-hatred. The bravado persona masks feelings of inadequacy and worthlessness that allow us to kill our brothers over insignificant disputes. It also allows Black men to put themselves in positions to be killed because of feelings of worthlessness and underlying depression. What appears to be homicide is essentially suicide. Disrespect is used as an excuse to become violent. Manhood is falsely equated with being able to beat someone down or pack a 9mm. *Gangsta* rap violence perpetuates this and some can't distinguish between fantasy entertainment and reality. We must put forth the same energy and relentless focus on stopping the Black-on-Black crime in our communities as we did in stopping white men from killing us.

Antisocial Racial Identity Confusion (ARIC) is a diagnosis I define as when an African American male identifies with a *gangsta* persona as a way of feeling powerful and strong. This bravado attitude masks underlying feelings of insecurity and powerlessness. It can also be a way of rejecting society's norms and values because of the belief and perception that society rejects Black males. This belief and perception is based on reality, but the resulting behaviors are maladaptive and self-destructive. Antisocial racial identity confusion (ARIC) is a form of self-hatred because it typically leads to victimizing other Black males and demeaning Black women. Killing other Black males, selling drugs in your community to Black children and mistreating Black women are all forms of self-hatred associated with ARIC.

Growing up in the hood, I witnessed many similar challenges, especially when I would return home from college. There were times when I would come home and hang out with my friends from the block. They were involved in *gangsta* activities, especially territory fights. One guy from another part of town was known for beating people up and as a "stick-up kid who pistol whipped people." His older brother had killed people.

One night some of the boys from my part of town instigated a fight between us. I was known to be strong because of my football career, lifting weights, and having quick hands. We were at a club where everyone was waiting for a fight to break out or some type of violence for excitement. This phenomena was heightened on hot summer nights. On this particular night, the two groups set it up for us to fight. I had thoughts of returning to school, the paper I had just completed and the new clothes that I planned to take back to college. That was my future. However, my indelible past placed me as part of the streets. When you live in a hostile environment, you remain in a constant state of defense to protect yourself and ward off predators.

The fight was on and as I began to get the best of him, he pulled out a gun. My friends ran. I stood alone looking down the barrel of a gun. As I backed away, I realized in that moment that my life was more important than a foolish defense of my ego, but my ego still wouldn't let me run. I looked him in the eye and slowly walked away. I believe that if I had shown fear or run, I would have been killed that night. It was a major turning point in my life. I realized that I could have not only lost my life, but lost my dreams and for what? So I could prove that I could physically beat another Black man? I have lost my cousin, John, and four of my childhood friends to murder: Chris, Pete, Mel, and Rodney. One was shot in the back, two were shot in the head, one was killed in front of his children, and one was hung from a tree by a rival gang.

John and I were more than cousins; we were best friends. One of our favorite things to do was go to his mother's house and eat her delicious food. My Aunt Katie is like a second mother to me and my cousin Josie is like a sister. In high school, John ran track and I played football. We were each other's #1 fan and constantly encouraged one another.

When I went to college our lives began to turn in different directions. John had always assumed the role of physical protector of me and I tried to protect him emotionally by steering him away from trouble. He turned his life around and was doing well but trouble found him, and he paid for it with his life. There are times when I suffer from survivor's guilt because I believe that if I hadn't gone to college, John wouldn't have been murdered. However, it comforts me to know that before he died, John shared with his mother that he had turned his life over to God.

My friend, Chris Love, was shot in the head by a neighborhood friend over a petty argument. However, I believe it was underlying envy, which is our Achilles' heel as a people. Chris was an intelligent, up-and-coming activist who was completing his Ph.D. He and I would often meet at the library during semester breaks and motivate one another. If Chris were alive today, I am certain he and I would be writing this book together.

The *gangsta* mentality must stop!

This book offers alternative and healthy, productive ways to grow strong and powerful.

FREEING YOUR MIND – Slavery is like a form of Post Traumatic Stress Disorder (PTSD) and could explain some of the challenges you're experiencing in your everyday life. Although we are well into the twenty-first century, Black people are still dealing with the residual effects of slavery, racism and stereotyping. The anger and frustration over these conditions affects how we function on a daily basis. Some of us have even become preoccupied with these negative traumatic events and this stops us from being productive. This condition can be so debilitating that it prevents us from properly functioning and communicating in society.

If you find that you're obsessing about these issues, try reading more about our history and looking for stories that empower you. Don't just stop at slavery—move through to our accomplishments. This will help you transition from a feeling of helplessness to a sense of pride.

HAVING CHILDREN IN WEDLOCK – When we look at the problems that face our communities today, a lot of them are directly related to the destruction of the Black family. The majority of our Black children are born into homes where the father is not present. This hurts the children involved and our community at large. Boys need a strong male role model to usher them into manhood. Girls yearn for the comfort, protection, and affirmation of their fathers. Besides that, you deserve all of the joys and woes that come with being a father. It becomes more difficult *(but not impossible)* to tend to a scraped knee, to be active in your child's school PTA, to participate in early morning feedings, and to witness his first step in a single parenthood setup.

Don't make babies if you're not ready for fatherhood. If the woman you're with is not your wife (although she should be), at least protect yourself and her from an unwanted pregnancy and a sexually transmitted infection. When you do find "the one," cherish that woman enough to marry her *before* the two of you become parents.

HONORING OUR WOMEN – Let's treat our sisters like African queens. They deserve it. They are our partners, mothers, grandmothers, daughters, girlfriends, lovers, confidants, wives, teachers, work colleagues, and best friends. By mistreating them—physically and verbally—we disrespect ourselves and our heritage. When we were stolen from the Motherland, our sisters were right by our sides. We had an unspoken agreement that we would protect each other and that pact still holds.

When you're talking about a sister, think about the women in your life. You wouldn't want someone mistreating your mother. But upholding our sisters isn't only about what you say; it's also about standing up for them when other brothers disrespect them. If you don't allow your friends, family, or colleagues to denigrate sisters in your presence, the negativity will stop with you.

PUTTING YOURSELF IN THE OTHER PERSON'S SHOES – If we practiced this one habit, our lives would improve tenfold. It's important that we closely look at our actions to determine how they impact other people. Self-centeredness demonstrates a lack of maturity and is in direct conflict with His teachings. Just think how lost we'd be if God didn't put Himself in our shoes. The whole premise of Christianity is based on God's willingness and ability to walk in our shoes. Christ was able to understand us better, gain an appreciation for our challenges, and have compassion for our shortcomings. He requires no less of us.

RAISING THE BAR — Explore your life for opportunities to improve. It can start with something as basic as having your car cleaned on a regular basis, raising your performance at work, upgrading your appearance, cutting back (or eliminating) profanity, and just taking pride in everything that you do.

In *Your Best Life Now*, the author Joel Osteen, writes, "People of excellence go the extra mile to do what's right, not because somebody's watching them, not because they have to, but because they are honoring God." Find an opportunity to honor God on a daily basis and He'll never miss the chance to show His gratitude.

Now that you've reviewed my list, make a list of your own. Commit to making a change. Determine how you plan to put these good habits in play. As the Nike commercial commands, "Just do it!"

DRUG DEALING ➪ PRISON = MODERN-DAY SLAVERY

Prison is a billion-dollar business in America and it is sponsored by drug dealing fools in poverty-stricken neighborhoods. Poverty is the greatest challenge for the African American male since slavery;. Drug dealing is a symptom of inner city sickness inflicted by poverty. Most people who sell drugs start out glorifying other drug dealers in the community. It's no wonder drug dealers are the heroes in the neighborhood. But once you start selling drugs, you realize that things aren't the way they seem. The whole idea of making money, becoming a so-called *gangsta*, and living the "good life" is a lie. Most people don't make a "good living" selling drugs. In fact, they're just barely surviving.

That's unfortunate because many lives are destroyed as a result of a venture that is doomed to fail from the onset. These so-called "heroes" are a source of embarrassment for the community. The image of them running from the cops like cowards is deplorable. There is no pride in it. These drug dealers could excel in jobs using their minds, but instead, they spend their day corrupting their own communities. It's really a shame.

Someone with whom I grew up and knew very well was a drug dealer. He would often stay awake two or three days at a time working the block, but he wouldn't put in a day's work for a legal employer. If he had put the same energy into something positive, he could have become an entrepreneur. Unfortunately, we'll never know his true potential. He was shot twice during his drug dealing days and his last bullet was fatal.

I say live life the way God wants you to live and you'll get your reward. If you stay committed to any job for a few years, you and your income will continuously grow and you will progress on a professional and spiritual level. There are no shortcuts to success. Many have tried to make a beeline for money and power but they either ended up in jail, dead or wishing they were dead. Let's be committed to truth and stop the madness. That's the only way we can truly begin to heal our community and ourselves.

LOOKING TOWARD THE FUTURE

Do you describe a glass of water as being half empty or half full? Your perspective is important because how you view the world can have a great impact on how you deal with the challenges that lie ahead of you. Instead of focusing on the things that hinder your progress, I'd like to encourage you to think about the opportunities that are available to you. Don't count the doors that are closed. Instead, be thankful that God will leave at least one open for you. Focus on the many blessings the Lord puts before you.

Let's not thwart our attempts to succeed at things because of all of the negative reasons we create. Take a lesson from many of the people who are born in other countries. Their perception of the reality that surrounds them is very different from what we believe here in America. Let's just say that there are ten doors of opportunity before you and you immediately see that five of those doors are closed. We African American males are often so angry about the five that are closed that we don't attempt to open the remaining five. Maybe the next three doors are also locked but that fourth one could be open. People born outside of the United States are often from certain environments where nearly all of the doors are shut. Even after they face the first doors that are closed, they remain excited about the possibility that a few may be open. Their mentality and mindset enable them to persevere in the face of adversity and that enthusiasm alone can help shape a positive outcome.

So, while I'm not asking you to ignore racism, class status or any of the other ills that plague us, I am telling you that there is a silver lining in every situation and focus on that. Don't let anyone stop you from pursuing your dreams. Be aggressive and go after what you want. Allowing racism to hold you back is giving power to the evil people and institutions that perpetuate it. Racism is based on using power to oppress. It can put road blocks in our path, but we determine if we will allow it to stop us. If your progress is impeded by systemic challenges, identify the challenges, strategize a plan, and implement methods to address it. We cannot afford to allow racism to interfere with our mission and goals. You must change your thinking.

It is normal to experience periods of frustration, disillusionment, and even hopelessness. Acknowledge them but then rebuke them. Refuse to allow negative thinking to defeat you. Self-destructive behaviors are often used to escape or self-medicate as a way of avoiding the pain of racism. Rage is difficult to manage and sometimes leads to self-destructive actions such as drugs, womanizing, and gambling. Engaging in these behaviors may temporarily feel like a release from pressure, frustration, or stress. However, it is damaging to the mind, body, and spirit. Don't be a puppet that allows an oppressive system to pull your strings and provoke you to act in ways that destroy your dreams.

Strength takes insight and perseverance. Be strong and courageous in confronting self-destructive behavior and racism. Have insight into when it's better to ignore pressure and stay focused on the prize. Choose your battles wisely. Being assertive and direct is typically the best approach. However, there are times when it is best to keep your ego intact and ignore it. You know you are the man and could effectively destroy your oppressor with intellectual fortitude and physical strength. You could plan a strategic attack. But this would be investing energy and time in counterproductive ways. For example, if you are trying to catch a plane and a racist cab driver won't pick you up, you could chase him down to confront him or take down his cab number and report him to the cab company. Both would take time and distract you. Determine whether you have time to report him or focus on getting to the airport on time.

Focus leads to self-determination. You determine who you are and how you will react. Self-determination is taking power over how you respond in any given situation. A strong ego allows you to maintain self-respect even when someone is attempting to disrespect you. Their definition of who you are does not define you or determine what you will do. Don't allow anyone to set you up by creating a circumstance where they expect you to do something self-destructive. If a racist police officer decides to target you "driving while Black" and relates to you in a condescending and demeaning manner, don't allow his action to lead you to do something harmful to yourself. You may have visions of slapping the racism out of him but this would only exacerbate the situation. It is more productive to be relentless in reporting him and documenting his actions in a descriptive way that has potential harm to his career. No matter the outcome, no officer wants documentation in his or her record or an internal affairs investigation.

Discrimination has left residual effects, such as influencing some Black men to use racism as a crutch and excuse not to take responsibility and power over their lives. There certainly is racism in employment, education, and housing. However, let's break the patterns of allowing it to be debilitating. Disillusionment only leads to defeat. Eliminate thoughts of inadequacy and counteract institutional racism with pride and dignity. Racism is insidious and ingrained into the culture. This makes it confusing to know who the perpetrators are, at times.

Black scholars have termed this experience, "healthy paranoia." Due to this dynamic, Black men often do not trust systems. Have faith that your ability to discern will lead to good decision making. Racism is like a social communicable disease that spreads and affects us all. Oppression caused by institutional racism can influence some Black men to feel that they do not have a place in society. Because of this feeling, they are immobilized with helplessness. Don't allow these external factors to control who you are and what you do. With enthusiasm and determination, you can gain power over your life. Develop an internal locus of control. Instead of allowing external racist situations to dictate your actions, you determine your behavior.

EDUCATION REPARATION

*It's so taboo as to be unspeakable in most circles of American
life
Offensive altogether to many blacks and most of those white
And so we've kept silent, kept it chained in our guilt laden
throats
Leery of reprisal, ridicule, and shame*

Dare I say it? Come on now.

*The reparations word, seems to some absurd
Conniving, unseemly, like some sick wanna be verb
Fraudulent, and undeserving of the time it takes to mouth it
But upon closer examination, it's clear America's blatant
procrastination
Ought to be written about, screamed about and discussed
calmly*

*This is not about blame, but it is about healing
Healing and patching a divide that leaves in its wake
Open wounds and psychological despair
And while we as a people continue to prosper and persevere
We are leaving a glaring work undone*

*Education should be free for us, in recognition, as reparations
for us
For the descendants of those forced to endure the brutal hard
ships of
The Middle Passage.*

— **Larry Toussaint Garlington**

CHAPTER FIVE

Sunshine Sweetens Your Fruit: Creating Joy and Happiness Through Relationship & Family

PART ONE: RELATIONSHIPS WITH WOMEN

SUNSHINE SWEETENS YOUR FRUIT: ASSESSMENT STATEMENTS I

Not at all				Very much
1	2	3	4	5

1. I have healthy relationships with women.

2. I consider myself a protector of women.

3. I demonstrate respect and love in my actions toward women.

4. I control my tongue (yelling, cursing, name-calling) when upset with women.

5. I assume leadership at appropriate times in my relationship.

SUNSHINE SWEETENS YOUR FRUIT: PERSONAL INVENTORY I

1. Past issues affect my relationship by:

2. Women in my life love when:

3. When I feel hurt by a woman I:

4. My relationship with God affects my relationship with women by:

5. I can improve my relationship with women by:

NOTE: You will find inventory questions throughout this book. Please take advantage of the space left open to you to jot down your own notes and personal thoughts as you move through the text. You may find it helpful to review your notes from time to time to assess your progress or revisit an idea at a later date.

CONFESSION

I raised the roof and chased the cat
Brushed aside feelings that in the end mattered most
Alienated and shredded every fiber of love
While ego tripping along the corridors of bachelorhood
That was my way, I kept my feelings at bay and sacrificed my
good spirit
For the victory: The short-term promise of acute gratification
For the conquest: The nightly escapades that rendered me
famous (infamous)
And while I believed myself happy
It was all a figment of my "single," "unhitched" imagination
The truth of the matter is;
I only ever found happiness, when love inexplicably found me
Now I know the value of, the true value of reciprocity
I love my wife! For all of the reasons specified.
And more

She's rich: *In the soil, you know, the soul, inside and out,*
through and through.

She's forgiving: *My lady knows all there is to know. She loves*
me for what I've become and what I strive to be.

She's spiritual: *She loves her God. Faith is her sole proprietor.*
The anchor to which she attaches her very being.

She's reciprocal: *A natural giver. She validates me in terms*
that are empowering and uplifting.

She's honest: *She listens in meaningful ways. She speaks the*
truth, as she knows it. The most trustful person I know.

She's family oriented: *She's of the mindset that difficulties and joyous occasions should never be endured or enjoyed alone. The quintessential wonderful woman. She plants seeds and cultivates them in her home.*

She's passionate: *Fierce in her convictions. And beautifully and appropriately dramatic.*

She's loyal: *Betray me not, leave me never. I've learned to respect my woman. She taught me this.*

She loves me: *Amen!*

— **Larry Toussaint Garlington**

And the LORD God said, it is not good that the man should be alone;
I will make him a helpmate *(Genesis 2:18).*

THE BENEFITS OF MARRIAGE

If someone were to ask me why a young, handsome, strong man
with a lot of potential doesn't want to get married, I'd say that
young man hasn't been told about the true joys of a healthy marriage. By now, he's heard plenty about the benefits of being single but, for the most part, Black men aren't bragging about holy
matrimony. It's a shame that marriage is not promoted because
there's nothing better than having a strong, supportive mate to
greet you at home.

The man working on Wall Street who's dealing with a glass ceil-
ing would truly benefit from the knowledge and assurance he
could receive from a devoted wife. After battling in the board-
room, it would be nice to end the day with a woman who could
love him, caress him and build his spirit.

I know there are a lot of men reading this who are stunned. "I've
never heard anyone talk to me in this way," you might say to a
friend. Well, I'm telling you this because it's the truth. Two heads
are better than one and it truly is not good for man to be alone.

THE BIGGEST LIES
ABOUT SINGLE LIFESTYLE

Whether they admit it, most men realize that being single is not
what it's hyped up to be. Researchers report that single people are
not as happy or as healthy as their married counterparts. Singles
also tend to lag in income, lack emotional well-being, and die at
an earlier age than people who have tied the knot. Despite a long-

standing belief, single men don't get nearly as much sex as married men do. And unmarried men are more likely to suffer from mental health issues, alcoholism, and other types of illnesses than their married counterparts.

So why aren't Black men marrying? It seems the truth has yet to catch up with the lies. In an *Essence* article, Black men tell why they aren't marrying. Here's what they had to say and why I don't believe these reasons are valid:

Reason #1: **You don't have to marry a woman to get sex.** Brothers, I know for a fact that the best sex is when you are married. Sneaking around, running around, and having quickies can't measure up to having a wife who wants to turn you on and set the mood for your perfect pleasure. Living life in the fast lane can be exciting but it's also dangerous (particularly in this era of STDs, HIV and AIDS). Besides that, the women involved in non-committed relationships are being hurt. For me, dating this girl and that girl got played out quickly. I always felt guilty and was never happy because the women I was seeing wanted more and I could not fulfill their hearts or mine.

Though you don't have to marry to get sex, understand that a married woman is often ready to blow her husband's mind if she is treated right.

Reason #2: **You can get the same benefits of marriage by living with a sister.** Can you really? When you're married, you don't have a woman who is angry about doing things for you. In a non-married, live-in situation, women aren't really happy if their true desire is commitment. They know they are being used and manipulated. And let's face it, can you really be happy living with a bitter woman? You're living with an emotionally distressed person and that has to affect you in some way. When your home environment is off balance, you're stressed out and worried. It's a miserable existence.

Contrary to popular belief, living together doesn't get you closer to the altar. In fact, it may drive you further away. People who are truly interested in marriage understand that matrimony is more than living together; it's about making a commitment before God. That's why cohabitation could never be a substitute for marriage, it's the opposite. The two of you don't have a real commitment and can opt out at any time—and that's not a marriage. A marriage is a longstanding commitment where the two of you are focused on how you can stay together, not break up. This type of relationship brings out the worst in both of you if there isn't a plan for commitment.

Reason #3: **You don't want to marry just to get divorced and lose out financially.** You will never build those finances without your wife. Once you marry, you automatically have a stronger financial package. Your credit improves. And when you go in as a team to a creditor, you fare much better as a couple than you would as singles. You can build so much more with your wife.

You really shouldn't marry anyone if you're already thinking about breaking up. Even though it's true that half of all marriages end in divorce, don't forget the other half of couples that actually stay together. That could be you, if you aim for it. Don't think of marriage in financial terms, it's so much more than that.

Reason #4: **You aren't ready to have children—yet.**

Waiting to become a parent is a good thing. Be financially ready when you do become a father. But getting married does not mean you have to become parents right away. In fact, those first few "childless" years that you and your wife spend together are a special time. They allow you to build financially as you strengthen your relationship as a married couple.

When you do decide to have children, get married first. If you marry a woman with children, be ready to be a father. Your children deserve that and so do you. If a child is conceived from an unplanned pregnancy or there is a divorce, try to be involved in your child's life. Some mothers will sabotage this if you don't want a relationship with them. The reality is you may have to wait until the child is old enough to understand the circumstances. Then, communicate directly with the child and let him/her know that you will always be there for them.

Please don't be one of those bitter brothers who can't deal with another brother raising your child. If a man loves your child and is parenting daily along with their mother, he is their father too. Share the challenges and blessings.

I appreciate that my wife and I are parenting as a married couple. It sends a strong message to our children and to the world around us. Children know that you are committed to them as much as you are committed to each other. As for me, I enjoy being a part of something much bigger than myself. My wife and my kids confirm that my presence makes a difference. Nobody wants to start dinner until I get there. When I do come home from work, they are genuinely excited about it. That makes me feel special.

If you never give yourself the opportunity to become a husband and father, that's a feeling you'll never know. Even if you're a single man with a harem, that can't compare to your wife, kids and even the dog eagerly awaiting your arrival.

Reason #5: You fear that marriage will require change.
It will change your life but it will change your life for the better. You'll still have some time for the *homies*, but you'll probably be participating in more positive activities. For instance, instead of hanging out at the club, my buddies and I take both of our sons skiing. We still watch the game together with a few Heinekens but now it's much better because my wife will cook up a feast. We look forward to the catfish, ribs, collard greens, lasagna, shrimp, and the whole nine. You better believe that everyone comes to my house for the Super Bowl and we plan to have a blast. I reciprocate when my wife has her sister-friends or colleagues over. Darlene likes to go to the spa with her mother, best friend, Karyn and our daughter, Dotti. It makes me feel great when I make the arrangements and surprise her.

So things do change, but they change for the better. When I was in college, we'd hang out half the night. There is a time and season for that. If you are in your late twenties, thirties, and forties, there is something wrong if your lot in life is to be the last man standing at the nightclub. Your body can't handle that and even if it could, you have too much at stake to do those things at this point in your life.

Marriage does require change but that can be a good thing, particularly if it motivates you to mature and realize your potential.

***Reason #6*: You're still waiting for your perfect soul mate.** There is no perfect soul mate. Soul mates work daily on improving their relationship. A soul mate enhances you and you make her a better person. Men need to provide for and protect their soul mates. I realized that my wife was my soul mate when it was clear that I wanted to protect her and take care of her. Darlene is a very independent and accomplished woman who is extremely capable of taking care of herself. But I wanted to shelter her, soothe her and lighten her burden. From my perspective, she had always needed to be strong and take the lead. I wanted her to have options and someone to lean on. The moment I saw her emotionally vulnerable, I knew I had fallen in love with her. All I can say is that it was instinctual and intense. The intensity of my yearning to support her and give her her heart's desires makes me want to live another day. I need her. Yes, I need her. She is the rib that God took from Adam. Symbolically, the woman who is your soul mate should complete you. Darlene inspires me to be a better man and I want to work hard to provide for her and our children. Darlene always has my back and wants the best for me. She supports my dreams and encourages me. We were good friends for many years before we dated. In fact, she initially wouldn't date me because of our years of friendship.

Try to find someone with whom you can be friends and can accomplish things. You will inevitably have conflicts. Having differences is part of any relationship. The key is learning how to manage your differences. Because Darlene and I are both very assertive and leaders, we often both want to control things. Being married to a strong Black woman requires compromise and negotiation. Remember, soul mates work on improving their relationship daily. Ask yourself some important questions: Can we work on a project together and perform well? Can we build a home together? Can we raise kids together? Am I the right fit from a spiritual perspective? Is the person someone I can hang out with? Is this someone I can grow old with? Do we laugh and have fun together?

I can't tell you to stop waiting if that's what you want to do. But just be sure that the person you're waiting for really exists. Sometimes we use the "waiting game" as a way to hide behind the fact that we're afraid of commitment.

Reason #7: **You're really not pressed about getting married.** I believe that the key to becoming more successful and powerful is in the family unit. Again, you will become a much stronger person with your wife. You'll also seek out joy and happiness and have a stronger connection with the Lord. I don't believe the greatest happiness can be reached alone. For example, when you go to see a movie, you can't tell me that you'd rather go solo than share those funny moments with someone you care about. We are social beings and don't function as well in isolation. You can achieve your greatest sense of happiness and joy with a mate.

Unlike women, men aren't pressured by society or their families to marry. So in your view, you might have all the time in the world to get hitched. Well, maybe. But according to the Bible, marriage is the only way for a man to be made whole. According to *Genesis 2:24*, "Therefore shall a man leave his father and his mother, and shall cleave unto his wife: and they shall be one flesh." Your suitable partner is the only one who can complete you.

Reason #8: **You don't want to marry a woman who**

already has kids. It's a funny thing about kids—they're loveable whether they are biologically yours or not. Thank God he made it that way. Kids love you regardless of your bloodline and you can love them equally. Women who have children and are single have gained a level of respect for men who treat them right. They will appreciate your support. You will find that many women with children are much more understanding and appreciate men more. And you can learn from some of their struggles and wisdom.

But what you may not realize is that you can also enjoy intense love, care, concern, and joy for a woman who has mothered kids by another man. Your bond can be just as strong as if you actually had children together. God allows us to love each other deeply, regardless of the terms of the relationship.

Through prayer and constant conversation with God, let him reveal whether this is the woman for you. If you believe that this woman and your relationship is God-ordained, then you must also know that this woman and her children are a package deal. As your love for her grows, your love for her children will grow as well. And if God has truly picked this woman for you, then he will also provide you with the solutions to all of the questions you have in your spirit. If however, this woman is not "the one," set her free so she can find someone who will love her the way that she deserves.

***Reason #9*: You want to get your financial house in order before you get married.** This is a good idea. As a man, you will bear a large part of the financial responsibility when you marry and so you should have stable employment before you cleave to a wife. Before God created Eve for Adam, he gave Adam a job. And although his only responsibility was to name the animals, it was still a responsibility that he had to take on before he was provided with a life partner. At the same time, know the difference between wanting to prepare yourself financially and making excuses. Have specific financial goals in mind, plans on how you are going to reach those goals, a timeframe, and then take action. If there is a special lady in your life, communicate your plans to her, and if she's the one, she'll stick around, assuming your timeframe is reasonable.

To determine the right marrying age for you, look at your entire life. Sketch your life out and think about where you want to be and how you want to get there. Then, find a woman who is on the same page as you are and work toward your common goals.

Maybe you don't have concrete examples of successful marriages. Or, perhaps the men you hang out with have turned you against marriage. Don't listen. Most people make fun of things they fear or they try to hold you back because they don't want you to leave them behind. Think about the life that you want to design for yourself and then get down to doing it. Putting the statistics aside, if you want to be a real strong man, you need to think about family. Having a wife will fulfill you in ways that your single escapades never could.

So now you know why marriage *is* for you. But if you still need convincing, know that "living single" has become a sickness in our society and in the Black community. Here's why:

A man who is alone, or unmarried, is incomplete. Our heavenly father made Adam's helpmate, Eve, from one of Adam's ribs. The Lord took a rib from Adam's chest so that he could produce one of Adam's kind. Eve, a woman, was specifically designed for Adam to love, cherish, honor, and build with. From the beginning, marriage was God's will for our lives. Respect the institution of marriage as God's way. By staying single, you have not found the helpmate that God has specifically created for you and you can only be made whole by marrying the right partner.

A single man is at a disadvantage emotionally and intellectually. Two heads are better than one when dealing with the battles of this world. That team approach is so much more powerful and effective than trying to solve problems single-handedly. In a basketball game, if you are playing against two people by yourself, it would be extremely difficult to beat them, even if your skills are superior because there is strength in numbers.

Two people who work as partners can share thoughts and views in order to strategize and develop plans to achieve individual and collective goals.

Marriage keeps the Black family intact. Married people live longer so this alone helps preserve the Black family. As we discussed previously, marriage in the Black community leads to healthier, happier and wealthier Black people overall. Black men who are married are less likely to take risks and are more likely to be productive, law abiding citizens. Most importantly, our shift away from the family structure has resulted in an increase in the number of babies born to unwed mothers, a problem that began to worsen significantly in the 1970s.

Since 1960, the percentage of babies born to unwed mothers has increased more than sixfold. In 2002, more than two-thirds of Black births were born out of wedlock. Kids who grow up in single-parent homes are more likely to be single parents themselves, more likely to get in trouble, and more likely to grow up in poverty.

Children who grow up in single households are more likely to be poor. Research shows that children born in households where the parents are divorced or never married are more likely to live in poverty. In fact, the majority of children who were born in recent years that have grown up in single-parent households have experienced at least one year of poverty. This is an African American tragedy caused by us.

Children who grow up in single households are at risk. When you look at the kids who are on drugs, in jail, or have become teenage parents, the vast majority of them come from single-parent homes. Although many of our women do an excellent job as single parents, they shouldn't have to shoulder the burden alone. Having a household with two parents is beneficial in child development. We owe it to our children to provide them with all the tools they need to succeed and that includes a two-parent household whenever possible.

Healthy marriages build self-esteem and promote stability among the family members. If we could compel everyone in our community to commit to a healthy relationship, we would solve a substantial amount of the problems that plague us. It's unfortunate that there aren't more people speaking out on the sacredness of marriage.

I wish many of our popular stars would highlight the positives of being in relationships. By constantly telling people that they should be single, the very people who are supposed to be our role models are doing Black people a great disservice.

So what does this all have to do with you? By committing to God under the institute of marriage, you are not only carrying out His will, you are putting yourself in a position to excel and realize your full potential. You are serving as an example to other brothers who wonder if marriage is for them. Every marriage that works is proof that marriage can work and we need these examples to counteract all of the rhetoric that society promotes as a means to minimize the institution of marriage.

If you still don't believe that marriage is for you, what then? Consider not having children. If you don't think the woman that you're dealing with is "marriage material" then how could you allow her to be the mother of your child? But more importantly, your children deserve to have a two-parent home. If you're truly not ready for that, then you're not ready to have children. Be careful that a woman may want to have a child, even if you make it clear that you do not. At the very least, use a condom every time you have sex.

You owe it to the women that you're with to tell them the truth. If you don't want a commitment, effectively communicate that at the beginning of the courtship (before sex) so there are no hurt feelings later on (understand that there may still be hurt feelings but at least try to minimize them by being honest). Also, there are women who, like you, aren't interested in being serious and those are the women you need to be involved with. If you are currently seeing a woman who wants a relationship and you don't, let her go. She deserves the full package.

ARE YOU RELATIONSHIP-READY?

Answer these questions to find out.

1. Do you know what she needs in a relationship and have you discussed it?

2. Does she know what you want in a relationship and have you discussed it?

3. Do you have natural chemistry and attraction between the two of you?

4. If you are sexually active, do you have good sex that is frequent and enough for you?

5. Do you share reciprocal affection?

6. Are you both committed to serving the Lord?

7. Do you pray together?

8. Are you emotionally intimate?

9. Do you enjoy spending time together?

10. Are you happy together?

11. Are you able to resolve conflict without hostility?

12. Can you accept her the way she is without trying to change the core of her personality?

13. Can she accept the way you are without trying to change the core of your personality?

14. Are you comfortable with helping to improve each other?

15. Do you address issues and problems in your relationship?

16. If there is a problem, are you committed to going to premarital counseling?

17. Do you realize that relationships aren't perfect but there must be a good foundation?

18. Do you feel like you can't live without her?

19. Is she part of your destiny?

20. Does your union make you a better person?

21. Have you discussed your family history and any problems stemming from it?

22. Is she your soul mate?

23. Do you agree on a plan for your future regarding: a) children; b) careers; c) spiritual/religion; d) social; e) extended family; and f) finances?

If you have answered "no" to any of these questions, you need to focus on that particular area and be able to answer "yes" before you make a commitment.

UOICE OF EXPERIENCE #10

Ed understood that Carla was self-conscious about her weight. Her self-deprecating remarks really bothered him. He prayed and asked the Lord to help him support her and show understanding. Although he had empathy for Carla, he also felt frustration that she didn't seem to take steps to address the problem. After reflection and prayer, Ed started listening to Carla and validating her feelings. He would say, "I know you feel bad about your weight and I understand." He wouldn't try to solve the problem, he would just listen. After listening, he was able to ask her to think about how he should help her. Ed always wanted Carla to go to the gym with him and in the past he would

*try to persuade and even pressure her. With the changes in
Ed's approach, Carla was able to tell Ed that she didn't
feel comfortable going to the gym and even felt embar-
rassed around the thin women in their tight workout gear.
Ed was able to listen and validate Carla's feelings again,
showing genuine empathy. Carla asked him to take walks
with her. Ed agreed and offered to purchase bicycles.
Carla felt supported and they began to walk and go biking
together. Ed felt good about motivating, loving, leading,
and protecting Carla.*

MARRIAGE: KEYS FOR SUCCESS

Family is the fundamental cornerstone of human civilization and
marriage is the glue that keeps families together. This is especially true for Black families. When you look at our community, you
see a definite increase in the ills that plague us, such as teen pregnancy, crime, and violence when our marriages either decline or
fail to exist altogether. As a first step, I'd like to provide suggestions to those of you who are married, so you'll stay married.
Then, I ask that you pass these keys of success to other brothers
who are either married or seriously thinking about it. Although
the secrets to building and preserving a long-term marriage may
vary, depending on who you ask for advice, I think the following
recommendations are fairly universal:

PUT GOD FIRST: As the male, God has ordained you to
be the leader of your home. But what does that mean? It
means that you stand as God's representative in your home,
where you bear the responsibility to teach, instruct, inspire,
and motivate your wife and children to learn and obey
God's word as outlined in the Bible. The only way for you
to know the Bible is for you to study it. Further, your
responsibility as the husband is not only to direct your fam-

ily's path but also to lead by example, showing your dedication to the Creator on a daily basis.

KEEP IT REAL. At times, some husbands become disillusioned with marriage because their wives don't measure up to the fantasy that they have conjured up in their minds. But your wife was never meant to live up to your fantasy any more than you're required to live up to hers. Your ideal woman may be the perfect housewife, a sports enthusiast, a sexy love goddess, and a Bible-toting Christian all rolled into one. But your real-life wife may only have some of these qualities. She is meant to be your helpmate, sweetheart, inspiration, partner, lover, and someone with whom you can share your hopes and dreams. It's really not important that she's not perfect as long as she is perfect for you.

KEEP IT HONEST. Can couples overcome adultery? Sometimes. But why risk it? Trust is one of the most important factors in a successful marriage and once you violate that, it's hard to get it back. Cheating, however, is just one way to break trust. Keep no improper secrets and hold no grudges. Even when we tell little white lies we slowly chip away at our unions. Your marriage can overcome anger but when the trust is broken, it may never repair.

WORK AT YOUR MARRIAGE. We invest in our job and even in our hobbies, so we should invest at least that much effort toward the success of our marriage. One way to accomplish this is to participate in our marriage as God has commanded us to do. That requires that the two of you study the Bible, regularly pray for the success of your marriage, study other sources to enrich your marriage, and make a commitment to yourselves and each other to stay together for the rest of your lives.

BE KIND TO EACH OTHER. Every time you insult each other, call each other names, and say harsh things to each other, you unravel the fabric of your marriage. If you continue on this path of destruction, your marriage will fall apart completely. It's very important to be kind to each other, to love each other deeply and to always treat your wife as your sweetheart. As the saying goes, you can draw more bees with honey than you can with vinegar. Use honey when dealing with your spouse.

COMMUNICATE FREELY, FREQUENTLY AND SWEETLY. Let your spouse know that you always have time to hear what she has to say and if you are busy, make time. The last thing the two of you need to do is take each other for granted. Then as you communicate, make sure that you keep things positive. If there is something that bothers you, focus on the issue.

Don't make it a personal attack. And talk about how it makes you feel; don't take shots at your spouse. For example, you might say, "I feel frustrated when you are running late for dinner with my mother. I would like for you to be on time." Notice that this statement focuses on how the speaker feels and concludes with the speaker making a direct request. It doesn't attack the other person or mention things in the past that don't have anything to do with the matter at hand.

For example, it would have been counterproductive to say, "You are always late. That's why you are having trouble at work and I know you don't like my mother. Well, she doesn't like you either. I can't believe you were late again ..." There are at least four other issues going on there not relative to the discussion at hand. Stick to the issue. Remember that communication is a two-way street. It's not only about saying what's on your mind in a respectful way; it's also about listening to your wife.

DREAM TOGETHER. What does the future hold? Talk about it together, dream about it together, and then work together to make those dreams come true. If you dream together, you'll both have a stake in your dreams and you'll both work hard to make those visions a reality. Sharing your most personal thoughts helps the two of you create intimacy, which strengthens your bond.

BECOME ONE. When you took your vows, you were told that the two of you would "become" one flesh, meaning that the "joining" of husband and wife is an ongoing process. You do this by doing things together as a team. Practice thinking and feeling in unison. Solve your problems together. Raise your children together. The more things you do as a team, the deeper your love will grow for one another and you will begin to understand why you need each other.

GIVE WITH YOUR WHOLE HEART. Part of your responsibility as a spouse is to figure out all of the ways that you're going to make your spouse happy on a daily basis. According to the scriptures, God instructed you to do so. *Ephesians 5:28; 29* reads: "He that loved his wife loveth himself. For no man ever yet hated his own flesh; but nourisheth and cherisheth it, even as the Lord loved the church."

Love your wife in the same way that you would love yourself. The way one pastor explained it, "If you were cold, you wouldn't wait two hours to put on a jacket or sweater, you would do it immediately. By the same token, you are charged with dealing with your wives' needs as soon as possible." Besides, the Bible tells us that it is better to give than receive. Though a surprise kiss or hug requires little effort on your part, it might mean the world to your spouse. Asking, "How was your day?" goes a long way in terms of showing you care. In most cases, the more you give, the more you get. And giving, after all, is what marriage is all about.

PRACTICE FORGIVENESS. Part of your responsibility as a Christian is to forgive other people, as you would have God forgive you. But as a husband, forgiveness is absolutely essential for keeping your union intact. Don't sulk, brood or vow to get even. It simply does more to destroy your marriage than it does to save it. Saying you're going to "get even" only hurts yourself because your lives are intertwined.

Forgiveness frees you to be the best person that you can be. Holding on to things destroys the health of your relationship and your own physical health. For help in this area, pray and think about Jesus Christ. When Jesus lay nailed to the cross after being tortured, he simply stated, "Father, forgive them for they know not what they do." If Jesus can forgive under those circumstances, certainly you can forgive your spouse.

ROMANCE EACH OTHER. A friend of mine tells his wife, "How you got me is how you keep me." That's his way of letting her know that he doesn't want her to change from the woman that he dated. Although he never says it, the same rules should apply to him. He should continue to court his wife, impress her, and win her over because romance is a required ingredient throughout courtship and through marriage. Once the romance dies, the marriage may shortly follow. It's easy to let the demands of work, family, and other responsibilities get in the way of your marriage but that's definitely not what God intended. Your spouse should be a priority in your life; only God comes before her. Thus, it is your divine order to do whatever you can to maintain a healthy relationship and that includes keeping the flames of your romance burning strong. Plan new and exciting things to experience joy and fun together.

TRY EVERYTHING TO SALVAGE YOUR MAR-RIAGE. Your goal in getting married is to stay married. If God is at the center of your union, then nothing can destroy it because the Bible says, "What therefore God hath joined together, let not man [divide]" *(Mark 10:9)*. In fact, if you take it a step further, the two of you are forever connected because once you marry, you become one flesh. If you look at marriage as a permanent fixture in your life, then you'll be more committed to making it work and inspiring your partner to do the same. However, you must be equally yoked and as a man you must be committed to taking on your responsibilities as a husband, provider, and spiritual leader.

Don't half step. Do everything possible to salvage a marriage and turn to God. When two people aren't able to work on a critical marital issue, the situation worsens. If one partner is unwilling to turn to God or work on problems, the willing partner will suffer spiritually. Your relationship with God should guide you. You cannot force another person to grow or change. Sometimes divorce is inevitable. Turn to God for forgiveness and learn from the experience.

As you review the above suggestions, ask God to help you incorporate all of these "keys for success" so that you and your spouse can unlock a world of possibilities and happiness in your marriage. Most importantly, ask God to strengthen your commitment to your vows and to your spouse so that you can do exactly what He has commanded you to do: "Husbands, love your wives, just as Christ also loved the church and gave himself for it" *(Ephesians 5:25)*.

Sunshine Sweetens Your Fruit: Creating Joy and Happiness Through Relationship & Family

PART TWO: FATHERHOOD

FATHERHOOD: ASSESSMENT STATEMENTS II

If you don't have children of your own, think of the children in your life when considering these statements.

Not at all				Very much
1	2	3	4	5

1. I have healthy relationships with my children.

2. I consider myself a protector of my children.

3. I demonstrate respect and love in my actions toward my children.

4. I control my tongue when I get upset with my children.

5. I teach and model good values to the children in my life.

FATHERHOOD: PERSONAL INVENTORY II

*If you don't have children of your own, think of the children
in your life when answering these questions.*

1. My childhood experiences affect my parenting by:

2. Children in my life love when I:

3. When I feel disappointed in my children I:

4. I motivate my children by:

5. I teach my children discipline and structure by:

6. I inspire love for learning in my children by:

7. My relationship with God affects my relationship with my children by:

8. I can improve my relationship with my children by:

*NOTE: You will find inventory questions throughout this book.
Please take advantage of the space left open to you to jot down
your own notes and personal thoughts as you move through the
text. You may find it helpful to review your notes from time to
time to assess your progress or revisit an idea at a later date.*

FATHERHOOD

What makes the man? When is it his hour
When does his innate sensibilities burn ever bright
When before us, does he cease to think of himself
When does his undisputed greatness erupt in plain sight

When he looks down now, he looks down upon the one
Down upon the one who has truly changed his life
He prays, gives thanks, offers testimony
As testament for the single most cherished gift
Life.

Lessons to be passed on, paternal instincts to rely on
He's blessed with an openness, an affability heretofore unseen
He's willing; he's growing now, and married to the belief
That the sanctity of fatherhood reigns supreme

When a man becomes a father, he completes the cycle
He is no longer just a son, but guardian and counsel
He's reached his zenith, scaled the good mountain
And got it right, in God's eyes

— **Larry Toussaint Garlington**

VOICE OF EXPERIENCE #11

Calvin realized that the bills were really stressing out his girlfriend, Sherry. He admired her strength as a single mother, working and going to school full time. Sherry never asked Calvin for money, but he wanted to help. At first she was reluctant, but Calvin saw the genuine appreciation and respect she had for him. It inspired and motivated him to want to provide for her. He felt good when he bought groceries and took her 10-year-old son shopping for clothes. Calvin had never felt so focused with any other woman. He knew that it worked for him and Sherry. Some of the other women he dated had expected him to pay for things. Others felt insulted when he offered. He and Sherry understood each other on a deeper level and the chemistry and spiritual bond between them made their relationship work. They gave to each other and their caring was reciprocal. Calvin knew that he would work a second job to be there for Sherry if he had to.

VOICE OF EXPERIENCE #12

John was constantly on his son Johnnie about his homework and grades. Johnnie just wouldn't focus and concentrate. He was more interested in hanging out with his friends and shooting hoops. John disciplined him, yelled at him, and even hit him in anger a couple of times. One day, on a day off from work, he sat at the kitchen table with Johnnie when he came home from school. This direct attention and praise changed their relationship. Johnnie seemed to be able to concentrate and complete his assignments. His grades improved that week. John realized that Johnnie needed more attention and support from him instead of criticism and discipline. He was able to spend more time with him, guiding and reviewing his work. This love, leadership, and protection helped Johnnie to improve academically.

THE FATHER IN YOU

Becoming a father has been one of the greatest experiences of my life. Many men fail to realize the value of becoming a father because they've come from broken homes or particularly difficult situations. But when you miss out on fatherhood, you miss out on the opportunity to understand the true measure of God's love. As a good parent, you personify God to your children. You reach a level of growth and maturity that you will never experience anywhere else. When I think about the love I have for my son, there almost aren't enough words to describe it because it is just that deep. One Saturday afternoon after working out, I was nearly famished. I was really looking forward to eating that piece of leftover steak that I knew was waiting for me in the refrigerator but as soon as I was ready to take my first bite, I noticed my son eyeing the plate I had left on the counter.

"Can I have that piece of steak?" he asked. Believe it or not, as soon as he asked that question, the hunger automatically left me. There was no way I could eat that steak if I knew he wanted it. My desire to make my son happy is the most important thing in the world for me. As long as his belly is full, I'm content. Before I got married, I hated getting up in the morning. Now, I wake up fully alert because I have to get my son ready for and drive him to school. And it's the same enthusiasm with my daughter. If she needs me to pick up a paper for school that she left at home, I'll drive miles to give it to her because I want her to know that she means that much to me. It's important to me that even if I am at work or busy, they know they can count on me to put them first. I also want them to know the depth of my unconditional love and devotion to them.

As I indicated earlier, my father and I never had the opportunity to bond the way that I would have liked or deserved. Because of this, I am particularly sensitive to developing a strong relationship with my children. I dedicate a large part of my time conducting workshops that provide Black men with strong leadership skills so they can effectively become better fathers to their children and, in particular, help their sons make smooth transitions as they develop from boys to men. The response to this work has been overwhelming. But more importantly, lives are being changed as a result and I am proud to be a part of the process. In the workshops, I encourage men to commit to the women in their lives by getting married. As a first step in my workshop, I invite my male participants to say a pledge. I think it's important to publicly confess your intentions because it holds you accountable to yourself and other people. I also invite you to say a pledge. If you want, write down a list of your parenting objectives and create a pledge of your own. You can also use the one at the end of this chapter either as a guide or as your own pledge. The important thing is that you commit to keeping the promises that you make and apologize when you fall short.

Though my hope is for all Black children to grow up in two-parent homes, I understand why this has been a challenge for us. When we arrived in America on the slave ships, one of the first things the auctioneers wanted to do was break up the family. They did this because they understood how important family is to an individual's success. When you fracture the Black family, you damage its roots, making future development and growth nearly impossible. The effects of this abomination have been passed on from generation to generation but because the family unit was such an essential part of our African existence, we still yearn for it even when it is not a part of our reality.

Brothers, you have a profound impact on your family, whether you are present or not, whether you know it or not. Take an active role in your children's lives. They are depending on you and you owe them your best effort. Be a father to your children and you'll reap more blessings than you can ever fully imagine. Your active presence in your children's lives will have a life-long effect on them. You'd be surprised to learn how many grownups still crave a happy childhood. Dr. George Edmond Smith, author of *More Than Sex: Reinventing the Black Male Image* (Kensington, 2000), admits that his father's absence not only affected his childhood but also influenced his self-esteem, male-female relationships, and other areas of his life as an adult. Unfortunately, Smith sees some of his issues in a significant number of his patients and he concludes that Black men participating in two-parent homes make a big difference:

> *There remains a critical need for both male and female Black children to experience responsible Black fathers who can help them discover who they are. These fathers must help their children grow up without succumbing to unhealthy outside influences and negative stereotypes. In order for our children to understand what it means to have a family, we have to show them how it is to be one.*

As the saying goes, if you're not part of the solution, you're part of the problem. I ask that we all look for ways to become part of the solution so that we can build the strong Black families that are as essential to our development as a race and as a nation. If you're looking for some suggestions to improve in your role as a parent, consider these:

BE PRESENT. This is the most important thing you can do as a parent. If you haven't been able to be available for your children in the past, put that behind you and start fresh today. Kids tend to love you at whatever point you're at in your development. It's not too late.

However, if the mother of the child is hostile and rejecting of your involvement, don't respond in ways that would hurt the child. You may have to wait until the mother is more receptive or the child is old enough to relate to you independent of the mother. In the meantime, keep your children in your prayers.

REVISIT YOUR CHILDHOOD. If you really want to relate to your kids, you have to remember what it means to be a kid again. Even if you didn't like the way you grew up, make something up. It's never too late to have a second childhood. Learn how to whip your son at his X-BOX games; check out your favorite cartoon; teach your daughter how to swim; go for a sleigh ride. And when your kid wants to go out and play, join him!

STOP BEING ANGRY. With all of the challenges that Black men face in this country, it's easy (and understandable) to be bitter at "the Man" and "the System," but what good does that do? Anger doesn't solve problems, but it may cause you to self-destruct unless you use that energy toward more constructive actions. As K. Thomas Oglesby put it in his book, *What Black Men Should Do Now: 100 Simple Truths, Ideas and Concepts* (Dafina, 2000), "Get mad, then get over it. Life is too short to waste your time and energy on its negative aspects."

RAISE YOUR CHILDREN TO BE FINANCIALLY RESPONSIBLE. As a good parent, it's important that you pass on good habits to your children. Do them and you a favor by teaching them about budgeting, taxes, credit, saving (pay yourself first), investing (get your kids in the stock market now), and savvy consumerism early in life. If you need some lessons on this, expand your reading (read the money section of the *Wall Street Journal, New York Times,* and other financial publications), connect with a good financial advisor, and collect tips from the next chapter in this guide.

TEACH YOUR KIDS TO DREAM. Dreaming is an expression of faith and demonstrates your belief in yourself. Regardless of what your parents taught you, don't pass on doubts or self-defeating thoughts to your children. Help them feel that everything they dream of is within their reach. That same faith will help them start a business, lose weight, or land a job when they reach adulthood.

IT'S YOUR MOVE

At this point, you have the tools you need to find the right mate and cultivate a healthy, loving relationship with your children. But the Bible says that faith without works is dead. In other words, you actually have to "act" if you want to get results.

FATHERHOOD PLEDGE

I PLEDGE TO COMMIT FULLY
TO HONORING, PROTECTING,
AND PROVIDING FOR MY FAMILY.

I WILL HONOR THE WOMAN THAT I
LOVE AND GUIDE MY CHILDREN.

I WILL SUPPORT, ENCOURAGE,
RESPECT, AND INSPIRE THEM.

DAILY PRAYER AND COMMUNION
WITH GOD WILL GUIDE ME.

I WILL PRAY FOR MY FAMILY AND
COVER THEM WITH MY FAITH IN OUR
LORD AND SAVIOR, JESUS CHRIST.

CHAPTER SIX

Money Tree: Nurturing Your Financial Power

MONEY TREE: ASSESSMENT STATEMENTS

Not at all			Very much	
1	2	3	4	5

1. I can describe what money means to me.

2. I plan for my financial future.

3. I manage and budget my money well.

4. I respect even small sums of money.

5. I believe I have the potential to be wealthy.

MOnEY TREE: PERSONAL INUENTORY

1. I believe God views money as:

2. When I hear, "Money is the root of all evil," I think:

3. My plans for financial security are:

4. I will be prosperous if I:

5. When I am having financial difficulty I:

6. Poverty is the root of all evil because:

*NOTE: You will find inventory questions throughout this book.
Please take advantage of the space left open to you to jot down
your own notes and personal thoughts as you move through the
text. You may find it helpful to review your notes from time to
time to assess your progress or revisit an idea at a later date.*

INSPIRATION

There is a passageway leading into the halls
Of success,

One that is never hidden, but very difficult
to place.

Though seldom traveled for fear of failing,
Those inspired will forever know the way.

The finest of gifts may linger in a soul,
Parade in its midst and never be found,

But when thoroughly searched for with the
light of inspiration,

The woes of defeat rarely sound.

— **Larry Toussaint Garlington**

BLACK MEN WHO FOLLOW THEIR FAITH HAVE A CHAMPION ATTITUDE

What do T.D. Jakes, Michael Jordan, and Bob Johnson, founder of BET, have in common? They are all Black men in America who have followed their faith, achieved their dreams, and become successful. The movie, "Ray," demonstrated how a man's roots or family of origin affect his psychological functioning. Ray Charles's mother was a powerful force in helping him overcome adversity. Our childhood experiences directly influence and impact our ability to pursue our goals. Dreaming is an expression of faith and demonstration of belief in yourself. You've got to believe in yourself.

The messages we heard in childhood can encourage or discourage us. If you heard positive messages, you will be inspired. If you heard negative messages, you will need to replace them with positive ones. Thoughts affect behavior. Dream and then the dream must be put into action. Don't get stuck in doubt and self-defeating thoughts. Cognitions affect our emotional state and behavioral patterns. "I won't be able to start a business" … " I can't eat healthy and get into shape" … "I'm not good enough" are all negative cognitions. Prayers and positive thoughts will direct our challenging life circumstances.

Going after what we want with passion and commitment is a champion attitude. Of course there will be setbacks, challenges, and obstacles. Take the hit but keep moving. When I played football, it provided me with a philosophy for life. Despite the pain, bruises, periods of defeat and jeering fans, an athlete has to maintain an attitude of winning. He must have a relentless pursuit of the goal. Sometimes you have to sacrifice immediate pleasure and diligently focus on a clear and detailed plan in order to bring your vision to fruition. There will be periods of feeling overwhelmed and tired. However with prayer, positive affirmation, and brotherly support, we can tap into our spiritual inner strength. For example, we can say "God is with me, I believe in myself, and my family and closest friends support me." During times of challenge, we gain insight and understanding into how to overcome problems.

Recognize that all champions have times of trials and tribulations, but champions are resilient and able to rejuvenate. A champion attitude doesn't depend on life circumstances. It is an attitude and positive outlook on life — bring what it may — we will succeed. It says, we are still in the game and willing to take the hits as they come. This attitude and focus allows us to keep moving down the field because we know one hit doesn't end the game. We turn to other plays in the book, alternatives to problems. Win or lose, we learn something from the game. In learning, we achieve something of great value. When you have the heart of a champion, even the most crushing blows can't defeat you. It is a philosophy of life that affects your ability to pursue goals. If you become aware of the depth of God's love for you, you will feel invincible and nothing will come between you and your divine destiny.

Black entrepreneurs such as Magic Johnson and 50 Cent don't wait for America to give them their forty acres and a mule. They aggressively fight for and claim their piece of the American dream for prosperity. If you have a champion attitude, racist institutions, and individuals fuel your drive toward your destiny. Plot and plan against prejudice with precision and turn your rage into weapons of mass determination. Although you can't control circumstances, you can control your response to them.

The key is the five Ps: PRAYER, Preparation, Practice, Patience, and Peak Performance.

1. **PRAYER** — Pray daily to increase your faith and pray specifically about your goals. Increase your biblical knowledge and understanding of God's word.

2. **PREPARATION** — Prepare yourself by knowing the game plan and plays. Know your goals and have a clear and detailed plan to achieve them.

3. **PRACTICE** — Practice the plays with discipline and focus. Do something every day that is a step toward your goal.

4. **PATIENCE** — Be optimistic and patient in pursuing your goals. It doesn't happen over night. All accomplishments take planning, discipline and time to achieve.

5. **PEAK PERFORMANCE** — Execute with excellence. Do your best at whatever you commit to.

VOICE OF EXPERIENCE #13

James wanted to start his own business. He had a business plan and goals, but James didn't have any savings. He could have tried to get a loan, which would have given him an opportunity. However, he also loved material things. He spent money on fine jewelry, a new car, and expensive clothes. He was unable to sacrifice immediate gratification for future gain. When he told his aspirations to close friends and family members, he began to hear similar feedback about his spending habits. Although he was hurt and defensive, James began to look at his lifestyle differently, which led him to cutting back on spending and focusing on ways to invest his time in earning money. He was able to gain information from the Internet on business opportunities. Although things did not move as quickly as he wanted, James was able to be more practical and realistic in moving toward his goals. He

*opened an investment program that he could not touch for
a period of time and was eventually able to start his own
business.*

VOICE OF EXPERIENCE #14

*Giving back to the community and taking care of his moth-
er were more important to Clyde than money in the bank.
He made good money and did not have a family so Clyde
believed he should help others. When his nephew did not
have enough money to go to the college of his choice,
Clyde was frustrated that he did not have enough savings
to pay for his tuition. At this point, Clyde began to rethink
his perspective that having too much savings wasn't right.
His view of money changed and he realized that it wasn't
"evil" or "bad" to be affluent. Clyde began to see money
as power and opportunity. This empowered him to work
harder, invest, and save in order to be a greater help to
others and to enjoy his life more. He began to allow himself to enjoy some of the privileges his money afforded
him.*

VOICE OF EXPERIENCE #15

(Sean "P Diddy" Combs, Record producer, entrepreneur
Excerpted from *Living to Tell About It* by Darrell Dawsey)

*I've seen a whole lot of people around me gain hope. The
nature of Black people most of the time is to just be jeal-
ous. But, what I've experienced and what I've paid more
attention to is how my success has motivated people to
have drive to go to school and achieve something.*

*My visions help other people have visions whether it is to
open up a store, go to school or get a regular job. Having
a regular job for Blacks is at the low point. With a regular
job, you're not the man as much as you might be being a
drug dealer or an athlete. And that's what society has
instilled in you. It's like Big, one of our artists, says in this
line: Either you're slinging crack rock/Or ya got a wicked*

*jump shot so you want to be either the best drug dealer or
have a wicked jump shot. For others, and myself, the
music industry has proved to be a strong outlet for Black
youth. Before, people wanted to be a rapper or a singer
but now people want to be an executive behind the scenes.*

There are many African American men— Earl Graves, Russell
Simmons, for example—who have successfully mastered
American economics and have been able to do very well financially. For the majority of us, there is still more to learn. In this
chapter, we'll uncover specific strategies that we need to use to
be competitive and financially successful under American capi-
talism. "Meditate on the Lord's commands day and night and you
will be prosperous and successful." *(Joshua 1:8)*

VOICE OF EXPERIENCE #16

*Jared tended to procrastinate in completing tasks at home
and at work. He always waited until the last minute to get
things done and this frustrated his wife and his coworkers.
Jared had waited to visit his grandmother in the hospital,
planning to go as soon as he finished a few things. His
grandmother died before he got there. Jared felt guilty and
depressed. He was angry with God but prayed for things
to change in his life.*

*Jared wanted less stress and pressure so he would be able
to complete things and not feel so overwhelmed. Nothing
seemed to change and Jared was frustrated with God. His
father gave him some of his grandmother's belongings,
including some of her books. Jared used his feelings of
pain as energy and fuel to motivate himself. Many of his
grandmother's books were religious and spiritual. Jared
read the books and took action. He gained faith in himself
and focused on developing self-imposed deadlines to complete projects at home and at work. Discipline and will-
power became critical to him. God did not change his circumstances. He still had stress and pressure at home and*

*at work but he asked God to change him. Jared made a
conscious decision to have focus and faith in achieving
goals. He finally conquered his procrastination, forcing
himself to complete tasks, even though he felt like relaxing
at times.*

TASKMASTER

So now that you know that you need money to secure economic
power, how do you plan to get it? Be a taskmaster. A taskmaster
is a person whose daily life and routine reflects steps toward their
goal and mission. He is so mission-oriented that he almost eats,
sleeps, and drinks his ambitions. He feels emotionally strong
when he is constantly moving toward his mission. He clearly sees
progress and results of his focus, like a pyramid rising from great
plinths toward the sky.

Your daily routine should involve listing and prioritizing the necessary steps in how to achieve your goals. As each step is completed, check it off your list and move to the next step. Each task
is important in completing the project. Track your progress in a
measurable way so you can recognize your achievements in a
concrete way. Be a taskmaster in moving toward your purpose,
practicing discipline and commitment along the way.
Consistently focus on your goals and objectives.

Being a taskmaster takes discipline. But you can do it if you
allow the Holy Spirit to guide you. Mentally and spiritually,
allow Him to take authority and power over your thinking. Resist
the temptation to be unproductive, even if it means passing on a
particular social activity. For example, I love to watch television
reruns of "Star Trek," but since those are episodes I've seen
already, I'd prefer spending my time completing a particular task
toward my goal. Practice removing emotional attachments to

unproductive behaviors. Concentrate and stay focused on the goal, despite feelings of frustration and disillusionment.

Resist the temptation to give up when you think your goals aren't being achieved fast enough. Know that God delivers in His own time. The more you trust in Him, the more patient you'll become. The key word here is patient, not complacent. Keep your eyes on the prize and keep charting a course for achievement.

Soon, you will find that your mind will gain greater power over your defeating emotional states. Strong will power will help you command authority over your life. This will facilitate actualizing your dreams. Action-oriented will power will make your dreams become realistic visions and bring them to fruition. You set the vision of what it is that you want to accomplish and achieve, and then have realistic, measurable goals of how to reach your vision. We must erase all the negative brain washing and stereotypes and replace them with our own positive thoughts and affirmations, saying that we will achieve, we will accomplish, and we are powerful. We will be taskmasters and deal with challenges and obstacles, and turn them into successful experiences.

To help you stay motivated, consider auditory stimulation such as gospel music, inspirational sermons, or self-improvement books (play CDs while you drive to work). Nix the negativity by staying away from people, places, and things that don't support your goals. When you hear negative statements, replace them with positive affirmations such as: "I am an achiever, I will accomplish my dream, I am powerful, and I am a child of the King of Kings." Set a schedule. Don't just list the tasks that you need to do each day, actually attach a time to them so you use your time effectively.

RESPECT MONEY

Money is not the root of all evil. The Bible actually says that the love of money is the root of all evil. Money can enable you to provide a stable environment for your family and give you security when you retire. It can be used as a means of opportunity for yourself, your family and community. Just think about how much we could advance our community if the entertainers, athletes, and successful entrepreneurs would donate a portion of their earnings to the struggle.

Our ancestors did just that. In 1853, Martin Delaney organized a Black economic development conference in Rochester, New York, to encourage cooperative economics. The objective was to convince Black people to start putting their money together for a common cause. Frederick Douglass pushed for this again in 1865 when he became chairman of the board of the Freedom Bank. Seventy-thousand Blacks made deposits in this bank over the next nine years.

By 1890, historians say Blacks had already started 31,000 businesses. In 1898, Fred Moore and Booker T. Washington launched the National Negro Business League, where concepts such as "Double Duty Dollars" and "Buy Black" were emphasized. Similar efforts followed, giving birth to enterprises such as Mutual Insurance in 1898 (one of the largest Black insurance companies), Mechanics and Farmers Bank in 1908, and the development of the Hayti Business District (a well established self-sufficient Black community in Durham, North Carolina, that boasted more than 150 Black companies). So money, when used for the right purpose, has served African Americans well.

Being stuck in poverty is the real evil. It robs you of your dignity and your ability to enjoy the fruits of our ancestors' labor. It clouds your focus, dampens your confidence, and hinders your ability to actualize your goals and dreams. Of course, people who are impoverished can overcome their obstacles and prevail. They go on to serve as an inspiration to others in their community. But, we should still avoid the cycle of poverty at any cost because people who lack financial resources have to focus on their day-to-day needs rather than betterment of the entire community. We need all hands on deck if we're truly going improve the state of Black people.

Since we made America wealthy with our labor, blood, sweat and tears, it only stands to reason that we should benefit from the proceeds. Let's see money for exactly what it is: a means to an end. Having money enables us to support the people we love and care for our families and communities. The power and control money provides will enable us to enjoy freedom (true freedom to control our destiny), authority, respect, and dignity. Use money as other groups do, according to Jawanza Kunjufu, author of *Black Economics: Solutions for Economic and Community Empowerment.* In his book, he writes, "Other races have developed an economic base and have hired politicians to represent and reinforce their economic interests. For some reason, African Americans want to build the political base before the economic foundation." Money will provide us with that foundation.

CREATING GOOD HABITS

There's no denying that racism and America's efforts to keep the Black man in bondage might occasionally dampen your spirit but those actions will never defeat you, especially if you're a constant work in progress. Take a look at yourself. Think about how people perceive you. Decide whether you exceed the expectations of your friends, family, coworkers, and bosses. Determine the types of emotions that come up when people think about your actions or interact with you. Do you like what you see? Even if you do, there's always room for improvement.

Only you know what good habits you need to institute in your life. Below I outline some behaviors that generally benefit *us*. See if any of them are useful to you:

BEING ON TIME. Brothers, being late with an excuse is not the same as being on time. It doesn't matter if you're late by five minutes or five hours. Being late, even by one minute, just isn't good enough. Imagine the prospective employee who arrives just fifteen minutes late for a thirty-minute interview, or the chef who overcooks a one-minute egg by only five minutes, or the passenger who arrives just one minute after the train pulls off or the heart doctor who enters the operating room only thirty seconds after the patient has passed away. Late is late!

Do yourself and the people you love a favor: Be on time. You can run ahead of schedule by putting an extra hour between appointments and leaving at least forty minutes early. Once you reach your destination, use the extra time to get a newspaper, mail a letter, get a cup of coffee, or make a brief phone call. You'll notice a big improvement in your life from this change alone.

CREATING FINANCIAL STABILITY. If you owe money to credit cards, car retailers, clothing stores, or any other source that you couldn't conceivably get money from, then you have debt. These expenditures of yours are helping to make other people rich, while good debt, like a house or stock, for example, helps to make you rich. Stop making other people rich and start investing in your own future.

To get out of debt, first determine how much debt you're in by opening the bills and actually taking the phone calls from creditors. Then make a list of your debts. If you're in good standing with any of the people or companies that you owe, ask for a lower interest rate or an extension. Then, start paying off the ones with the highest interest rates first. And pay more than the minimum, so you'll actually feel like your making progress.

Most importantly, start changing your habits. Keep track of what you spend and look for ways to reduce those expenses by distinguishing your wants from you needs. "Wants" can wait. If you're looking for areas to eliminate, stop eating out (or at least eat out less often). Buy "regular" instead of premium gas. Cut down on your entertainment expenses. While you're making changes, save credit card use for emergencies. Try paying off the balances in full every time you use them, and restrict your use to the major ones (that's all you really need). Be on the hunt for bargains, from toilet tissue to cars. Set up a budget and stick to it. This plan should include a means to pay you first, whether it is toward a savings account or other investment tool.

GOOD CREDIT. You get good credit by paying your bills in a timely manner. It's really that simple. From this point on, pass on a purchase if you know you can't afford to pay for the item in full in thirty days or less. In fact, eliminate the potential problem altogether by paying for things in cash whenever possible and by restricting your spending to things you really need.

If you already have bad credit, be proactive. Contact the three major credit bureaus — Experian, Equifax, and Transunion — to get copies of your credit reports. Closely examine them for accuracy. If there are mistakes, contact the bureaus to ensure those errors are corrected. Then contact the creditors to negotiate future payment terms. Stick to the agreement that you made and you'll be on the road to credit repair sooner than you think.

MAKE YOUR MONEY WORK FOR YOU. Knowledge is power, especially when it comes to making money and using it for your benefit. As an example, I didn't realize the significance of taxes until I moved into a different tax bracket. Since I grew up on welfare, we didn't have a tax bracket. But when I started doing my own taxes, things such as tax shelters had relevance. I was amazed how much money you can lose or save based on your tax bracket and how you manage it. I also acquired a lot of useful information when I acquired my first home. If it weren't for a good friend, I wouldn't have done as well. He told me how to apply for a mortgage step-by-step. This information not only made a difference for me but it allowed me to better provide for my family.

In addition, learn to manage your money prior to purchasing a home. Of course, your search for knowledge shouldn't stop here. I'm just scratching the surface with these tips, but if you apply them, you will definitely be on the path toward prosperity. Start taking these steps today:

PAY YOURSELF FIRST. Start this habit as soon as you can. Take a certain percentage out of everything you earn and deposit it into some type of investment tool. Be diligent about this and you'll reap the benefits later.

GET EDUCATED ABOUT MONEY. Go to seminars, read books and money management publications, watch

programs such as "CNN Money Watch" or listen to
Bloomberg radio. Join an investment club. All of these
resources will assist you in learning about money management and help you gain the confidence to establish your
own investment portfolio.

**SEPARATE YOUR NEEDS FROM YOUR WANTS
AND SAVE FOR YOUR WANTS.** Do you want a new car
or need one? If you have a car that works but isn't as nice
as you would like it, that means that you just want a new
car. Treat yourself to material things on occasion, but don't
let material things consume you. Put your purchases in perspective and resist the temptation to buy anything on
impulse. If you see a great deal, sleep on it before you make
the purchase. If you still want the item in the morning, it's
probably worth the buy. If you want the luxury car, plan and
save for it.

I sacrificed by driving my old car from college to save to
buy my Jaguar. Then, when I married Darlene, the time
came when she needed a new car. I saved and sacrificed
buying quite a few items I desired in order to buy her one.
When our daughter needed a car for school it was also a
time when we needed a truck due to the weather in the win-
ter. Dotti was uncomfortable driving a jeep or truck as her
first vehicle. Therefore, I suggested that Darlene take my
car, give Dotti her car and I would buy a used jeep. This sacrifice brought me great joy as a husband and father.

CONSIDER STARTING YOUR OWN BUSINESS.
There are some big pluses to owning your business: the
buck stops with you; you set your own work schedule; there
is a greater potential for income than a standard nine-to-
five; you control your destiny; you reap the tax benefits of

business owners; you may have the ability to employ your family and friends; and you have a greater ability to pass on wealth to your children. But entrepreneurship takes commitment, drive, leadership, long hours, greater responsibility, optimism, and endurance.

If you don't have those things (at a minimum), you might need to work for someone else. But if you do want to enter the arena of entrepreneurship, step out in faith with confidence and a clear action plan.

THINK OUTSIDE OF THE BOX. The next time you need something, ask yourself, "Can I make it? Can I borrow it? Can I buy it wholesale?" And if you answer "no" to these three questions, then ask yourself "Do I really need it?" In many instances, you'll answer "no" to this question too.

GET A HANDLE ON YOUR CREDIT CARDS. Credit card debt is unproductive. When you use a credit card, even a check sometimes, it doesn't feel like you're spending real money, but you are. In most cases you end up spending much more than if you would have used cash. So try to save your credit cards for emergencies or in cases where credit cards are the only acceptable payment (for example, a car rental or telephone transaction with the airlines).

When you use credit cards, make sure you make your payments in full and on time at the end of the billing cycle. If you use credit cards in this manner, you're actually able to take advantage of a free thirty-day loan. Now that's the smart way to use credit cards.

SET UP A MONEY JOURNAL. In your journal, record every penny that you earn and every cent that you spend (even if it's on a pack of gum). This will help you determine the areas where you waste money and enable you to eliminate spending in those areas.

VOICE OF EXPERIENCE #17

Kevin was newly divorced and feeling overwhelmed with his life. Work responsibilities, co-parenting, and family stress were all too much for him. His house showed his stress as there was clutter and junk all around. As Kevin began to look at his life, he recognized that if his environment and finances were in chaos, his thinking and life could not have order.

He took a long weekend and began to organize his house starting one room at a time. Balancing his checkbook, cleaning and putting things in boxes helped him to feel a sense of structure. He could find his keys and wallet much easier. His mind was clearer and he felt better about himself. Kevin added a structured prayer time to his schedule and his overall spiritual and physical health improved. These changes provided a daily sense of accomplishment. Kevin felt good when he came home from work every day to a clean house.

SHOW YOURSELF THE MONEY

You can make the American dream a reality for you. You can reach your financial goals. For success, you just need to use legitimate *(legal)* tools, rely on God for guidance, exercise discipline, do the proper research, and believe that you have the know-how to achieve your goals. It's as simple as you choose to make it. "I am the master of my fate, I am the captain of my soul" was written as a prophetic way of explaining that we control our destiny. Black men need to see money as part of our destiny. You deserve prosperity. If you desire wealth deep in your soul, you will go after it with relentless pursuit. You will focus your thoughts and energy on it. Don't fear success and ponder thoughts of lack and poverty. This mentality sabotages pursuit of economic gain. Intensify your desire for financial power. Know that financial power allows you to help others and to give back. Your purpose should be all-consuming with persistence and determination. A thought can be transformed into material gain.

Along the path to financial success, you will undoubtedly experience periods of defeat and failure. Get back up and keep moving toward your goal. Use negative experiences as stepping stones to success. Think abundance and think purpose. What would wealth afford you? What good would you do for your woman, children, and our community? God blesses so that we may bless others. Scripture says that to those who are given much, much is required. Develop a plan of action to achieve the financial success you desire. Desire will inspire and motivate you. Imagine your heart's desire and imagine sharing it with others. Dream your dreams and don't allow anyone to discourage you. Visualize being able to make your wife an African Queen and being able to give her gifts of love. Think about being able to afford the best education for your children. You can set up a computer lab in an underserved Black community.

Believe in yourself and your business ventures. Take initiative to go after your dreams. Put your vision and dreams into action. A plan should be implemented with purposeful actions. Don't allow fear to immobilize you. If you are afraid of financial success or its consequences, you will sabotage it. Some Black men are overwhelmed with the thought and responsibility of making financial decisions. They would rather not have money than to have to figure out how to manage it. The other extreme is living beyond your means to impress others.

- **Write down your financial goal.**
- **Repeat affirmations about prosperity.**
- **Rebuke negative thoughts of lack.**
- **Take daily steps toward financial goals.**
- **Visualize goal attainment.**

Emulate people who have achieved financial success. Study their history and formula for success. Be decisive in your plan and show leadership. Assume responsibility for your financial goals. Be willing to do all the tasks of a job you ask others to do. If you open a restaurant, be willing to wash dishes. Be prepared and disciplined for the position you desire. Education and experience will help you present in a knowledgeable and professional manner. Research the company that you are interested in ahead of time.

Demand your rights as an American to accumulate wealth. Our families need food, housing, and clothing like any other family. Money and wealth should be used for the good of the less fortunate, to motivate and inspire them, to teach them to fish instead of giving them fish. We live in a capitalistic country and we deserve our share of the American pie. America provides opportunity. Take it and focus on available avenues instead of closed doors.

There is nothing to stop you from developing a business. Patronize Black businesses and learn from successful entrepreneurs. If you allow your thoughts to focus on lack, fear, and frustration, you will not succeed. Positive thoughts, faith, determination, and action lead to financial success. Your dominating thoughts affect your subconscious mind and lead to actions. Plan a course of action. Acquire the background and knowledge to pursue your financial goals. If you want to open a bookstore, work in a bookstore first and learn the business. Work as a barber to open your own barbershop or do construction work in preparation for opening your own construction company. Develop a unique aspect that would be appealing to customers. Be open to God's guidance and direction. Choose a path to financial success that will be pleasing to Him.

CHAPTER SEVEN

Tree of Life:
Harvesting Your Divine Destiny

TREE OF LIFE: ASSESSMENT STATEMENTS

Not at all				Very much
1	2	3	4	5

1. I can describe who God is to me.

2. I have specific goals and aspirations for my life.

3. I have a plan to reach my goals and aspirations.

4. My goals will have a positive impact on other African American males.

5. I am committed to the improvement of my life.

TREE OF LIFE: PERSONAL INVENTORY

1. I am improving myself by:

2. I am improving the relationships in my life by:

3. I am improving my physical health by:

4. I show discipline in achieving my goals by:

5. I am putting God at the center of my goals and dreams by:

NOTE: You will find inventory questions throughout this book. Please take advantage of the space left open to you to jot down your own notes and personal thoughts as you move through the text. You may find it helpful to review your notes from time to time to assess your progress or revisit an idea at a later date.

TAKE ACTION: MOTIVATING BLACK MEN IN THE 21ST CENTURY

Despite the fact that racism prevails in American society today, you are capable of controlling your destiny. No one can "keep you in your place." You have the power to take control over your actions and decisions. Black men have a legitimate right to feel angry about the injustices perpetrated against our families. Take this anger and channel it into constructive action toward achieving your goals. Set a plan and stick with it. Don't allow yourself to become overwhelmed with oppression.

People who expect to achieve their goals don't sit still; they take the initiative and do something positive in their lives. Successful people seize opportunity, not tomorrow, not later on today, but this instant! However, the course to self-improvement may require you to eliminate some of the negative habits and people who have been taking up space in your life. Other changes may also require painful decisions and sacrifice, but the bottom line for you will be the satisfaction and personal growth that only comes with this process. It's clearly within your power to find the job or career of your heart's desire.

Many people may sincerely want to do things differently (the desire), and will make resolutions each year (the decision), but never take the steps necessary (the deeds) to reach their goals. The key to reaching any goal before you even try is spending time soul searching to find your reason why. To find your unique goal or dream, ask yourself why you are setting a given goal. In other words, how will you benefit by achieving it? Whom do you wish to help or empower? The answers to these questions can be used as constant motivators when you face the challenges that come as you strive to meet your aims. In fact, the more compelling reasons you have, the more powerful you'll become! Post these reasons in places you see often, such as the corner of your bathroom mirror and above your desk at the office. This will serve as a constant reminder of why you must and will ultimately succeed in your life.

An old saying suggests that you can eat an elephant one bite at a time. There's nothing made that can't be seen as the sum of smaller parts, from large projects to daily chores to your most cherished dreams. However, people frequently become paralyzed because they make their goals so unreachable that they become overwhelmed by their size. The key to accomplishing any task is to break it down into individual steps, then tackle each of those one at a time. By starting small, you make your goals more believable and attainable. Once you really believe you can achieve a goal, you're already halfway there.

Whether your goal is small or large, express success in tangible ways that you can measure, touch, or count so you can keep track of your progress. Ask yourself what it means to accomplish your goal (be it to lose weight, make money, or become successful). How do you personally define success? In other words, do you want to lose ten pounds or twenty pounds? Or maybe you want to make a thousand dollars, or a million dollars. Likewise, if you want to sell a product that markets for twenty dollars, just how many units of that product would you need to move in order to pay your bills each month?

Without specific goals for attaining your objectives with a quantifiable result attached to it, a goal is essentially meaningless, it's just "a wish." You can let that number quantify the goal you set for yourself. In this case, the more specific you can be in setting goals, the easier it will be to chart your progress and make your goals tangible realities.

A RECAP

Putting Your Personal Plan of Action Together

PERSONAL PLAN OF ACTION

1. Five things in my life I recognize the need to improve:

2. The first step I will take in resolving each of these five
    things:

3. The second step I will take in resolving each of these five
    things:

4. The third step I will take in resolving each of these five
    things:

5. If my first plan of action doesn't work, my second plan of
    action is to:

*NOTE: You will find inventory questions throughout this book.
Please take advantage of the space left open to you to jot down
your own notes and personal thoughts as you move through the
text. You may find it helpful to review your notes from time to
time to assess your progress or revisit an idea at a later date.*

You have gone through the process of examining your identity, developing self-love, relying on prayer, combating racism and self-destructive behavior, creating family joy, and developing financial power. Let's recap where we started and where we are now. Then, you will balance the different aspects of your life and pursue your goals with passion and determination.

– CHAPTER ONE –
UNDERSTANDING DEVELOPMENT
AND FAMILY OF ORIGIN INFLUENCES

KNOW WHO YOU ARE

Your ID = Spirituality + Family + Education + Social/Economic Status + Society's Effect on Me

First and foremost, accept yourself as a child of God and a Black man. The primary element that defines who you are is based on your relationship with Christ. Once you are confident about your role as a child of God, you will never be confused about your identity again. Stop being your own worst critic. Stand in front of the mirror, pat yourself on the back, and congratulate yourself for reading this book and starting this journey. Be your own best friend.

You can't live your life for other people, so don't even make that attempt. Instead, aim to make God and yourself happy; then, your family and friends. Don't be overly concerned about what other people think about you—that is their opinion. Learn to laugh to ease tension and express joy in who you are. Accept the things that you cannot change and attempt to change the things you can.

– CHAPTER TWO –
LOVE THY SELF

IMPROVE YOUR MIND AND BODY

When you love yourself, you can love others in full measure. If you don't love yourself, how can you expect others to see what a wonderful person you really are?

Perhaps it's time for an assessment and some changes. Improve your relationship with God and others. Improve your health. Improve your mind. Improve your appearance. Improve your prospects. It's all connected, but first you have to get started.

Turn off the television and pick up a good book. Likewise, you can attend a lecture or an interesting play today. Enroll in a class or two at a local college or business school. Focus on learning more about Black history and our proud legacy and traditions. Read a newspaper on a daily basis. Subscribe to any publications that specifically discuss your industry.

Following consultation with your physician, create a personal exercise routine. Actively participate in your exercise plan by walking, jogging, swimming, bicycling or weightlifting. Re-evaluate your diet and adopt a more nutritious diet plan and stick with it. Seek professional help for this purpose, if necessary. Get a new haircut or buy a new suit. Treat yourself to a relaxing body massage or a few minutes in a hot sauna. You deserve to rejuvenate and recharge your batteries. We men need to develop ways of relieving stress, tension, and anxiety.

– CHAPTER THREE –
RELYING ON THE POWER OF PRAYER
TO CULTIVATE YOUR PURPOSE IN LIFE

TAKE CONTROL OF YOUR DESTINY

Take the time to learn about your heritage. Overcome stereotypes. Work hard toward your own goals and dreams. Take pride
in your roots. Give back to the community and you will be
rewarded tenfold. Volunteering can be a very rewarding experience and there are so many opportunities to get involved. Making
a difference will strengthen your faith. Young Black men need
positive role models and it is important that you share your
knowledge and experiences.

DEEPEN YOUR FAITH

Meditate on the Lord's Word in the Bible, the wonders of the universe and what your place is in it. Explore God's purpose for your
life. Spend quiet time alone in prayer. Have faith in your ability
to achieve your goals and to fulfill God's plan for you. Thank
God for his blessings. Commit to giving, and make spirituality
part of your purpose in life.

– CHAPTER FOUR –
COMBATING OPPRESSION, RACISM,
AND SELF-DESTRUCTIVE BEHAVIOR

KEEP FOCUSED

Make a point to learn about the pitfalls and traps that you can easily fall into. Knowledge is power and the more you know about

the past and present forces working against you, the more prepared you are to handle them should they arise.

Make a commitment to elevate the Christian Spirit within our nation, our countrymen and ourselves. Share your enthusiasm and ideas, always with your divine destiny in mind.

AVOID THE NEGATIVES

Self-improvement is not without sacrifice, but it's in your best interest to get rid of negative "friends." You don't need people in your life who are destructive forces. Furthermore, thoughts such as "I cannot," "I should not," "I must not" may be keeping you from getting what you want. Just as words have power, negative thoughts can actually make you ill. Whenever we are in a place where we don't belong, there is a little voice that says, "Run!" Listen up.

– CHAPTER FIVE –
CREATING JOY AND HAPPINESS
THROUGH RELATIONSHIPS & FAMILY

IMPROVE YOUR RELATIONSHIPS

Improve your love life if you are already in a relationship. Do an ongoing careful re-evaluation. Is your married life or relationship with a significant other missing something? Is there something you're not getting from it or something you're not giving to it? Identify the problem and the opportunity for change. Discuss with your partner what is needed and dedicate yourself to making the change today. Examine your relationships with your children and extended family members also. Pledge to be a better father.

Open up the lines of communication with coworkers, friends, and loved ones. If an old grudge or misunderstanding has been complicating your life, resolve the conflict with the person involved. This can be done by simply dropping it, talking it out or getting out of the relationship. Forgiveness reaps enormous rewards for the soul.

– CHAPTER SIX –
NURTURING YOUR FINANCIAL POWER

TAKE CHARGE OF YOUR CAREER AND FINANCES

Ask yourself what type of job or career would give you so much personal satisfaction that you would even do it for free. Check the employment ads or fill out an application or apply to college—to help bring about your heart's desire. You are always teaching, especially at your place of employment. Your job is a gift from God so treasure it. At the same time, if it's time for you to depart, leave on good terms.

Develop a routine that will help move you toward your goals. Frequently check your progress and reassess on a regular basis. Formulate a strategy that works for you. Talk to successful people and see how they reached their goals.

Make a personal budget, and start saving at least 10 percent of your monthly earnings. You will be surprised to see how fast your savings grow. This step cannot be overemphasized. Patronize Black businesses and solicit their support. Whenever you can, buy Black. It might require spending a few extra cents or driving a longer distance, but do it anyway. Tell your friends to do the same.

– CHAPTER SEVEN –
HARVESTING YOUR DIVINE DESTINY

SEIZE YOUR DREAMS AND GOALS

Make a list of your five most desired dreams or goals. then make a sub-list of steps to attain the dreams or goals. Each day write your goals in priority order and identify five things that you will do to work toward them. Check off each task as it is completed. Make a commitment to follow through and regularly assess your progress. Do it today. Do it now. These steps can make your life better and help you realize your dreams and goals.

FOCUS ON THE FIVE Ps

Review the Five Ps on page 160 and then put them into use: Prayer, Preparation, Practice, Patience, Peak Performance.

Ten Commandments for African American Males

1. Thou shall love JESUS CHRIST and follow his commandments.

2. Thou shall love thyself.

3. Thou shall be a full-time student and/or employed.

4. Thou shall marry the woman he loves.

5. Thou shall love, protect, and provide for your family.

6. Thou shall be your African American brother's keeper.

7. Thou shall pursue economic prosperity.

8. Thou shall support Affirmative Action and Reparation.

9. Thou shall pursue and support the empowerment of African Americans.

10. Thou shall be willing to sacrifice your life for these Commandments.

Meditate on the Lord's commands day and night
and you will be prosperous and successful.
— *Joshua 1:8*

ORDER FORM

Pass along the wisdom! To order additional copies of **"Roots of a Man,"** complete this form and send it, along with a check or money order for the amount of your purchase plus shipping and sales tax, to:

Ernest C. Garlington, Ph.D.
P.O. Box 597
Marion, CT 06444

Please send _____ copies of **"Roots of a Man"** at **$14.99** (softcover) or **$25.95** (hardcover) each to:

Name: _____

Street Address: _____

City: _____

State: _____ Zip: _____

Phone: _____ E-Mail: _____

Please include $4.95 shipping and handling
for each copy ordered.

To contact Dr. Garlington regarding speaking engagement availability, send your request to DrErnieG111@aol.com.